i Think: Reading & Writing

Literary Themes

By Kendra Corr and
Dr. Sue Vansant

 Atlanta, Georgia

** It is the goal of InspirEd Educators to create instructional materials that are interesting, engaging, and challenging. Our student-centered approach incorporates both content and skills, placing particular emphasis on reading, writing, vocabulary development, and critical and creative thinking in the content areas.

Edited by Sharon Coletti and Kendra Corr

Cover graphics by Sharon Coletti and Print1 Direct

ISBN # 978-1-933558-71-4

Printed in the United States of America

About InspirEd Educators

InspirEd Educators was founded in 2000 by author Sharon Coletti. Our mission is to provide interesting, student-centered, and thought-provoking instructional materials. To accomplish this, we design lesson plans with standards-based content presented in a variety of ways and used as the vehicle for developing critical and creative thinking, reading, writing, collaboration, problem-solving, and other necessary and enduring skills. By requiring students to THINK, our lessons ensure FAR greater retention than simple memorization of facts!

Initially our company offered large, comprehensive, multi-disciplinary social studies curricula. Then in 2008 we joined forces with another small company and author, Kendra Corr, and launched a second line of thematic units, some excerpted and adapted from our original products. These flexible and affordable resources are ideal for individual, small, or large-group instruction. We hope you will find our company's unique approach valuable and that we can serve you again in the near future.

If you are interested in our other offerings, you can find information on our website at **www.inspirededucators.com**.

InspirEd Educators materials provide engaging lesson plans that vary daily and include:

- Lesson-specific Springboards (warm-ups)
- Writing Activities
- Critical and creative thinking
- Problem-solving
- Test-taking skill development
- Primary source analyses (DBQ's)
- Multiple perspectives
- Graphic analyses
- Fascinating readings
- Simulations
- Story-telling
- Practical use of technology
- Debates
- Plays
- Research
- Graphic organizers
- AND SO MUCH MORE!!!!!

Thank you for choosing our units,
Sharon Coletti, President
InspirEd Educators

Tips for Teaching with InspirEd Educators Units

- Before beginning the unit, take time to look through the Objectives and lessons. This will give you a chance to think about what you want to emphasize and decide upon any modifications, connections, or extensions you'd like to include.

- Give your student(s) the Objective worksheet at the beginning of the unit study. The Objectives serve as an outline of the content to be covered and provide a means to review information. Have the student(s) define the vocabulary terms as they progress through the lessons and thoroughly answer the essential questions. You can review their responses as you go along or wait and check everything as a test review. It is important that your student(s) have some opportunity to receive feedback on their Objective answers, since assessments provided at the end of the unit are based on these.

- Read through each lesson's materials before beginning. This will help you better understand lesson concepts; decide when and how to present the vocabulary and prepare the handouts (or transparencies) you will need.

- "Terms to know" can be introduced at the beginning of lessons or reviewed at the end, unless specified otherwise. (In a few instances the intent is for students to discover the meanings of the terms.)

- Look over what we have given you and use whatever you feel your student(s) need. Suggestions are sometimes offered for enrichment, but feel free to use any lesson as a jumping off point to pursue other topics of interest.

- Our materials are intended to prompt discussion. Often students' answers may vary, but it's important that they be able to substantiate their opinions and ideas with facts. Let the discussion flow!

- Note that differentiated assessments are provided at the end of the unit. Feel free to use any of these as appropriate; cut-and-paste to revise, or create your own tests as desired.

- For additional information and research sites refer to the Resource Section in the back of the unit.

- InspirEd Educators units are all about thinking and creativity, so allow yourself the freedom to adapt the materials as you see fit. Our goal is to provide a springboard for you to jump from in your teaching and your student(s)' learning.

- ENJOY! We at InspirEd Educators truly believe that teaching and learning should be enjoyable, so we do our best to make our lessons interesting and varied. We want you and your student(s) to love learning!

Table of Contents

Literary Themes Objectives

Vocabulary - Define and be able to use the following terms:

- motif
- unconsciousness
- theme
- element
- underdog
- metaphor
- descendants
- prophecy
- characteristics
- initiation
- quest
- supernatural
- scapegoat
- legend
- journey
- trials and tribulations
- parapet
- civil war
- mentor
- philosopher
- ethics
- protégé
- archetype
- seductress
- nurture
- prologue
- star-crossed lovers
- inhumanity
- utopia
- dystopia
- American Dream
- civil rights
- allusion
- meek
- associate

Fully answer the following questions:

1. Explain what a literary theme is.
2. Describe the common elements of an underdog story.
3. Explain where hero stories often come from and what typically happens in them.
4. Explain typical journeys that occur in fiction and other literature.
5. Describe the common elements involved in coming of age stories.
6. Explain how characters such as mentors and female archetypes make stories more interesting.
7. Describe the star-crossed lovers theme.
8. Explain how themes such as utopia and the American Dream appear in literature and other works.
9. Explain the meaning and symbolism of Bible stories and color in literature and other works.

Literary Themes Objectives - Suggestions for Answers

Vocabulary - Define and be able to use the following terms
Definitions for terms are provided in the lessons in which they are introduced.

Fully answer the following questions:

1. *A literary theme is a unifying idea in literature and other works of writing or film. These broad ideas appear across various times, places, and cultures. Understanding the concept of themes allows the reader to recognize common elements in similar stories.*
2. *Underdog stories often adhere to a pattern similar to the David and Goliath story from the Bible. An underdog such as David faces a much more powerful foe like Goliath. Then against all odds the unexpected victor defeats his seemingly unbeatable rival, often with a symbolic weapon. In that particular story it is a rock which symbolizes the love and protection of the God of Israel.*
3. *Hero stories are often based on legends (such as Robin Hood or King Arthur). Generally, the hero has an unusual childhood, possibly raised by people other than his/her parents, lives in seclusion, has a mentor, and may even have some sort of supernatural powers.*
4. *Stories of the journey theme often involve characters going to fantastic places, sometimes with enchanted landscapes, difficult terrain, and magical or dangerous creatures. The character often takes the difficult journey as a quest, encountering and overcoming various trials and tribulations along the way.*
5. *Coming of age stories usually involve a character who transitions from childhood and innocence into adulthood. The transition typically occurs as a result of some jarring or traumatic event.*
6. *Many stories include older, wiser men or women who help the main character, who benefits from the mentor's special gifts or knowledge. Many other female archetypes also appear in literature, such as the temptress, nurturer, or waif. The inclusion of archetypes helps develop a story and makes it more interesting.*
7. *The star-crossed lovers theme involves a forbidden romance between two young people who are kept apart by background, warring or fighting groups (such as their families), or other factors, but who fall in love despite the rifts. In most cases these stories end tragically with one or both of the star-crossed lovers' death and tremendous grief among the remaining characters.*
8. *Both themes address society. Authors who create utopian societies in their works describe their ideas of perfect places where people live blissfully. American Dream stories and other works often focus on how people in society, regardless of their background, work toward success.*
9. *Allusions and symbolism add meaning to stories. Authors may use elements of Biblical stories to add dimension based on the common experiences of many of their readers. Colors are used to draw associations between certain shades and meanings; snow white, for instance, implies purity.*

Déjà vu All Over Again

Springboard:
The students should read "Psychology and Literature?" and answer the questions.

Objective: The student will be able to explain what a literary theme is and give an example.

Materials:
Psychology and Literature? (Springboard handout)
The Great Flood... (2-page handout)
Shared Stories (handout)

Terms to know:
motif - a recurring pattern through time and place
unconsciousness - the state of being unaware
theme - a unifying idea or subject of a story or other work

Procedure:

- After reviewing the Springboard, explain that *much of this unit will deal with the common motifs, otherwise known as "themes"* (review the term) *that are present in literature*. Go on to explain that *in this lesson the student(s) will do what Jung did: examine stories from various times and places to discover common motifs or themes.*

- Distribute "The Great Flood..." and "Shared Stories." The student(s) can work independently, in pairs, or small groups to read the stories and complete the matrix.
- Have the student(s) share and compare their findings and discuss the questions. *(Similar elements in all stories were: flood as punishment, righteous man and animals saved, etc. An example of a "theme" would be that "gods" punish wrongdoers with natural disasters, "gods" have ultimate control over humans' lives, "gods" forgive and bless those who follow their commands, etc.)*
- **EXTENSION:** Have the student(s) conduct research to find additional flood stories in other cultures.

Psychology and Literature?

The 19th century psychologist, Carl Jung's (pronounced Yung) interests were many including: astrology, the study of the effects the movement of heavenly bodies on people and events; alchemy, an early form of chemistry; and even literature. Jung was quite the **Renaissance Man**! Still, Carl Jung was best-known for his ideas about the mind and human behavior.

One of his most famous psychological theories was about a "collective unconscious," the idea that humans have all had similar experiences. These common pasts, he believed, influence our behavior and actions. Yet we act and think without understanding why we do what we do or why we feel as we feel. A baby, for example, cries when it's hungry but doesn't know why. Jung believed that throughout history, people have experienced similar events, situations, conditions, and interactions, leading them to act, react, and think in similar ways. He calls these shared experiences "motifs." Over time, Jung reasoned, the motifs became so common that they became permanently "stamped" into the minds of humans everywhere.

To support his theory, Jung compared the mythologies, oral stories, written histories, art, music, and poetry of many different cultures. He found that every group regardless of time or place had similar motifs! In some cases even the details were the same, such as names of gods, goddesses, settings, and events. He studied a wide range of civilizations from various time periods, ranging from highly educated to isolated and primitive cultures. Yet despite times and circumstances, the results were the same: civilizations share many of the same motifs.

The term "Renaissance Man" in the first paragraph **MOST LIKELY** refers to a person who

A. admires the artists of the Renaissance.
B. can create works of art or literature.
C. has a wide range of interests and skills.
D. makes a living as a psychologist.

According to Jung, "motifs" have all these characteristics **EXCEPT** that they

A. only exist in highly educated or advanced cultures.
B. are based on similar experiences among peoples.
C. contribute to why we act and feel the way we do.
D. become part of our "collective unconsciousness."

Give another example of something that Jung might consider a "motif."

____

____

____

____

Psychology and Literature? - Answers & Explanations

The 19th century psychologist, Carl Jung's (pronounced Yung) interests were many including: astrology, the study of the effects the movement of heavenly bodies on people and events: alchemy, an early form of chemistry; and even literature. Jung was quite the **Renaissance Man**! Still, Carl Jung was best-known for his ideas about the mind and human behavior.

One of his most famous psychological theories was about a "collective unconscious," the idea that humans all have all had similar experiences. These common pasts, he believed, influence our behavior and actions. Yet we act and think without understanding why we do what we do or why we feel as we feel. A baby, for example, cries when it's hungry but doesn't know why. Jung believed that throughout history, people have experienced similar events, situations, conditions, and interactions, leading them to act, react, and think in similar ways. He calls these shared experiences "motifs." Over time, Jung reasoned, the motifs became so common that they became permanently "stamped" into the minds of humans everywhere.

To support his theory, Jung compared the mythologies, oral stories, written histories, art, music, and poetry of many different cultures. He found that every group regardless of time or place had similar motifs! In some cases even the details were the same, such as names of gods, goddesses, settings, and events. He studied a wide range of civilizations from various time periods, ranging from highly educated to isolated and primitive cultures. Yet despite times and circumstances, the results were the same: civilizations share many of the same motifs.

The term "Renaissance Man" in the first paragraph **MOST LIKELY** refers to a person who

A. admires the artists of the Renaissance.
B. can create works of art or literature.
C. has a wide range of interests and skills. *
D. makes a living as a psychologist.

(While Choices A and B are often true of Renaissance Men- or women, the term is used to describe Jung after telling of his many and varied interests.)

According to Jung, "motifs" have all these characteristics **EXCEPT** that they

A. only exist in highly educated or advanced cultures. *
B. are based on similar experiences among peoples.
C. contribute to why we act and feel the way we do.
D. become part of our "collective unconsciousness. "

(The passage explains that motifs crossed time and levels of cultural achievement.)

Give another example of something that Jung might consider a "motif."

Answers will vary but could be similar to the baby example in the passage. For example mothers will defend their children; people marry and have families; worship, etc. Jung would have attributed these common behaviors and practices to shared experiences.

The Great Flood...

FROM THE GREEKS:

Zeus sent a great flood to destroy all people of the Bronze Age. Prometheus advised his son Deucalion to build a chest to save them from the rising waters. Everyone but Deucalion and his wife died, except for a few people who escaped to high mountains. The water swelled to such heights that the mountains in Thessaly parted. Deucalion and his wife, after floating in the chest for nine days and nights, landed on Parnassus. When the rains finally stopped, Deucalion made sacrifices to Zeus, and then he threw stones over his head, which became men. His wife also threw stones over her head, and these became women.

FROM THE HEBREWS:

God, was upset at the wickedness of man, so he decided to destroy all of the humans. Only Noah was a good man and found favor with Him. God spoke to Noah, instructing him to build a huge ark with three decks. Noah did as he was told and took his family of eight on board along with two of each kind of animal. For forty days and forty nights the floodwaters rose until even the highest mountains were under water. The earth was covered for 150 days. Then God sent a wind to recede the waters, and the ark came to rest on Mt. Ararat. After forty more days Noah sent out a raven, which kept flying around. He next sent out a dove, which returned without finding a perch. A week later he sent out the dove again, and it returned with an olive leaf. The next week, the dove didn't return at all, so Noah knew it had found land on which to perch. So, after a year and ten days from the start of the flood, Noah and the animals were able to emerge from the ark. He then sacrificed some of the animals to God. God, pleased with his sacrifice, promised never again to destroy all living creatures with a flood and gave the rainbow as a sign of this promise.

FROM THE BURYAT OF SIBERIA:

The god Burkhan advised a man to build a great ship, and the man worked on it in the forest for many days. But he did not tell his wife what he was up to, telling her instead that he was chopping wood. The devil, Shidkur, told the wife that her husband was building a boat and that she should refuse to board it. She was told to say to her husband when he struck her in anger, "Why do you strike me, Shidkur?" The woman followed this advice and called the devil to board the boat with her when she did so. With the help of Burkhan, the man gathered two of all kinds of animals except the Prince of Animals (possibly a mammoth), which considered itself too large to drown. But in fact the flood destroyed all animals left on earth, including the Prince of Animals, whose bones can still be found in the land. Once on the boat, the devil changed himself into a mouse and began gnawing holes in the hull, so Burkhan created a cat to catch it, and the ship was safe once more to carry them until the waters dried.

FROM ISLAM:

Allah sent Noah to warn people to worship none but Allah, but most would not listen. The people challenged Noah to show them what Allah would do about it and mocked him when, under Allah's inspiration, he built a ship. Allah told Noah not to speak to Him on behalf of wrongdoers; that they would be drowned. Then as Allah had told him, water began to gush from underground and fall from the sky. Noah loaded onto his ship pairs of all kinds of animals, his family, and just a few others who believed. One of Noah's sons did not believe and said he would seek safety in the mountains, but he was among the many that drowned. The ship sailed upon great waves until Allah commanded the earth to swallow the water and the sky to clear. Then the ship came to rest on Al-Judi. When Noah complained to Allah for killing his son, Allah scolded him, saying the son was an evildoer. So Noah prayed for forgiveness, and Allah heard his prayers and told him that he and his family would be blessed.

FROM THE SUMARIANS:

The gods decided to destroy all men. The god Enlil warned the priest-king Ziusudra (which meant "Long of Life") of the coming flood. Ziusudra was told to build a great ship and load beasts and birds onto it. Then violent winds came, and a great flood covered the earth for seven days and nights. Then Ziusudra opened a window in the large boat, allowing sunlight to enter as he bowed to the sun-god Utu. After landing, he sacrificed a sheep and an ox and gave thanks to the gods. As a reward for protecting the animals and the seed of mankind, Ziusudra was given eternal life and taken to the country of Dilmun, the land where the sun rises.

FROM THE MASAI OF EAST:

Tumbainot, a good and honest man, had a wife and three sons. When his brother died, he married his brother's widow as was the custom. His second wife then bore him three more sons before the couple argued and she went off to set up her own household. At the time there were many people populating the world, but most were sinful and did not obey God. Yet despite their sins, there was no murder until a man named Nambija hit another over the head. At this, God resolved to destroy mankind. Only Tumbainot found grace in the eyes of God, who commanded him to build an ark of wood and enter it with his two wives, his six sons, their wives, and two animals of every kind. When they were all aboard, God caused a great flood, drowning all the other men and beasts. The ark with Turnbainot and the others drifted for a long time, and they began to run low on food. When the rain finally stopped, Tumbainot let loose a dove to learn of the state of the land. The dove returned tired, so Tumbainot knew it had not found a place to rest. Several days later he loosed a vulture with an arrow attached to its tail feathers. If the bird landed, the arrow would hook on something and be lost. But the vulture returned without the arrow, so Tumbainot reasoned that it must have landed on a dead animal, rather than grass, so the flood must have receded. When the level dropped, the ark grounded on the great plain and all came out. As he stepped forth, Tumbainot saw four rainbows, one in each quarter of the sky, and knew that God was no longer angry.

Shared Stories

Culture	Characteristics	Events	Reason for Flood	Who/What Survived?

1. What are some of the similarities among the stories?

2. What would you say are some of the themes of the stories?

Everyone Loves an Underdog

Springboard:
Students should read "David and Goliath" and answer the questions.

Objective: The student will be able to describe and recognize the underdog theme in fiction and non-fiction.

Materials:
David and Goliath (Springboard handout)
It's ELEMENT-ary (handout)
Short Story Planner (handout)
Short Story Scoring (1/2 sheet handout)

Terms to know:
element - a basic, essential part of something
underdog - expected loser in a fight or contest; someone at a disadvantage
metaphor - comparison between two unlike things, describing one as the other (ex. love is a rose)
descendants - family members of a later time
prophecy - prediction for the future

Procedure:

- While reviewing the Springboard, explain that *the Biblical story of David and Goliath has become a metaphor for the little guy overcoming the odds and defeating a powerful foe. Such underdog tales are even often referred to as "David and Goliath stories*." Go on to explain that *all "David and Goliath" tales have three elements: a powerful foe, an underdog that defeats the foe; and the means by which the foe is defeated is a metaphor which stands for something else*. Have the students identify these elements in the Springboard story. *(David is the underdog, Goliath the foe, and the rock is a metaphor for the power of God.)*
- Distribute "It's ELEMENT-ary" and explain that *in this lesson the student(s) will analyze this underdog theme in both fiction and non-fictions stories and write an original short story surrounding that theme*. Have student(s) work individually, in pairs, or small groups to analyze the two stories and share their ideas. *(Answers may vary. Schindler is the David in the first story, because he's one man against a huge foe; Hitler and his Nazis are Goliath. The stone could be the love and compassion that Schindler showed his "children." In the Irish legend Balor is the Goliath figure and Lugh is David. The stone may be the prophecy that came true.)*
- Distribute the "Short Story Planner" and have the student(s) plan and write a short story including all three elements of the David and Goliath story.
- **For group instruction** have the students read their stories aloud and have others identify who or what represents the three elements of the David and Goliath story in each. **For individual instruction** have the student share his/her story and explain the elements.
- Then have the student(s) evaluate their work using the rubric provided.

DAVID AND GOLIATH

The Philistines set up camp on one side of the Elah Valley in preparation for war with the Israelites. King Saul and his Israelite army set up camp on a hill on the other side of the valley. The hero of the Philistine army was named Goliath, a giant of a man over nine feet tall. He carried a spear strapped to his back and wore bronze armor on his chest and legs. His chest piece alone weighed 125 pounds!

Goliath stepped forward and shouted across the valley to the Israelites, "I am the best soldier in our army. Choose your best soldier to fight me. If he kills me, our people will be your slaves. But if I kill him, your people will be ours." Saul's men heard Goliath's words and were **petrified**, so they did nothing. Goliath shouted his challenge to Saul and his soldiers every morning and evening for forty days.

One morning a boy named David heard Goliath's shouting when he visited his older brothers at the camp. The soldiers told him that the king promised a great reward to the man who could kill Goliath, so young David went to King Saul and said, "This Philistine is making fun of us and insulting our God. I shall go out and fight the giant myself!" The king told him he didn't have a chance against the powerful Goliath, but David explained that he had killed many wild animals while tending his father's sheep and was not afraid.

King Saul finally agreed to let him fight, put his own armor on the boy, and handed him his sword to use. David took off the armor and sword because both were too heavy and he was not used to them. Instead, he picked up his shepherd's stick, found five smooth rocks and put them in his leather bag. Then, with his slingshot in his hand, he walked straight toward the fearsome giant.

Goliath came towards David and as he got a better look at the boy, he began to mock him. "Do you think I am an animal? Is that why you are coming at me with a stick! Come on! When I'm finished with you I'll feed you to the animals!"

David answered, "You have come to fight me with a sword, but I have come to fight you in the name of the Lord. Today he will help me defeat you, proving to all that the Lord needs no weapons to save His people." Then David put a rock in his sling and swung it around his head. The rock flew out and hit the giant square in the forehead, cracking his skull, and the mighty Goliath fell into the sand, dead.

Which of these scenarios is **MOST** like the story of David and Goliath?

A. A boy gets picked on at school by a bully.
B. A woman sues a huge company and wins.
C. A man divorces his famous movie star wife.
D. A girl rides her bike across a dangerous bridge.

Which definition of "petrified" **BEST FITS** its use in the second paragraph?

A. turned to stone
B. become stiff
C. stunned by fear
D. deadened

In the story the rock symbolizes the

A. bravery of David.
B. power of the Lord.
C. strength of the army.
D. armor of Goliath.

DAVID AND GOLIATH – ANSWERS & EXPLANATIONS

The Philistines set up camp on one side of the Elah Valley in preparation to go to war with the Israelites. King Saul and his Israelite army set up camp on a hill on the other side of the valley. The hero of the Philistine army was named Goliath, a giant of a man over nine feet tall, carried a spear strapped to his back and wore bronze armor on his chest and legs. His chest piece alone weighed 125 pounds!

Goliath stepped forward and shouted across the valley to the Israelites, "I am the best soldier in our army. Choose your best soldier to fight me. If he kills me, our people will be your slaves. But if I kill him, your people will be ours." Saul's men heard Goliath's words and were **petrified**, so they did nothing. Goliath shouted his challenge to Saul and his soldiers every morning and evening for forty days.

One morning a boy named David heard Goliath's shouting when he visited his older brothers at the camp. The soldiers told him that the king promised a great reward to the man who could kill Goliath, so young David went to King Saul and said, "This Philistine is making fun of us and insulting our God. I shall go out and fight the giant myself!" The king told him he didn't have a chance against the powerful Goliath, but David explained that he had killed many wild animals while tending his father's sheep and was not afraid.

King Saul finally agreed to let him fight, put his own armor on the boy, and handed him his sword to use. David took off the armor and sword because both were too heavy and he was not used to them. Instead, he picked up his shepherd's stick, found five smooth rocks and put them in his leather bag. Then, with his slingshot in his hand, he walked straight toward the fearsome giant.

Goliath came towards David and as he got a better look at the boy, he began to mock him. "Do you think I am an animal? Is that why you are coming at me with a stick! Come on! When I'm finished with you I'll feed you to the animals!"

David answered, "You have come to fight me with a sword, but I have come to fight you in the name of the Lord. Today he will help me defeat you, proving to all that the Lord needs no weapons to save His people." Then David put a rock in his sling and swung it around his head. The rock flew out and hit the giant square in the forehead, cracking his skull, and the mighty Goliath fell into the sand, dead.

Which of these scenarios is **MOST** like the story of David and Goliath?

A. A boy gets picked on at school by a bully.
B. A woman sues a huge company and wins. *
C. A man divorces his famous movie star wife.
D. A girl rides her bike across a dangerous bridge.

(Choices C and D don't parallel the story at all. A is possible, but omits the "winning" against a stronger foe.)

Which definition of "petrified" **BEST FITS** its use in the second paragraph?

A. turned to stone
B. become stiff
C. stunned by fear *
D. deadened

(Saul's men were afraid, and only C addresses fear.)

In the story the rock symbolizes

A. bravery of David.
B. power of the Lord. *
C. strength of the army.
D. tarmor of Goliath.

(According to the story, a tiny boy defeated a giant because he had the support of the Lord, fighting in his name.)

It's ELEMENT-ary

DIRECTIONS: Read the stories and identify the three ELEMENTS of a "David and Goliath" story in each. Be sure you explain your ideas!

STORY ONE: Oskar Schindler

Oskar Schindler was a heavy drinker, a womanizer, and a member of the terrible Nazi Party during World War II. Despite his faults, he used his position to save 1,200 Jews from being killed in the death camps of Hitler's Germany. This man did not set out to be a hero; in fact the opposite is true. He was a businessman whose main goal during the war was to get rich by producing weapons and bullets for the German army using forced Jewish labor. Over time, though, he came to see those who worked for him as his "children." After seeing countless people killed in a Jewish settlement, he pledged to make a difference.

He used his position and social connections to save as many *Schindlerjuden* (Schindler Jews) as possible. The fortune he earned from his business dealings was all spent in bribes to Nazi officials to protect the Jews who worked for him. When he died, he was penniless, yet the Jews ensured that he was buried in a very sacred spot in Jerusalem, in the cemetery facing the Old Temple gates. This German Nazi not only saw that 1,200 *Schindlerjuden* were spared, but as many as 7,000 of their descendants owe their lives to him as well.

David - ____________________

____

Goliath - ____________________

____

The metaphor - ____________________

____

STORY TWO: Balor and Lugh

Balor was the king of the Formorians, a group of giants on Tory Island. He had one large eye that could kill anyone it looked upon. According to a prophecy, Balor would be killed by his yet unborn grandson. To avoid his fate, Balor locked his daughter Ethlinn up in a tower to keep her from having a child. However a suitor was able to sneak into the tower and Ethlinn had triplets months later. Balor threw the babies in the sea but one, Lugh, was saved, raised by a foster father, and as a grown man became a great soldier.

Years later, Lugh led an army against the Formorians. He hit Balor in the eye with a sling stone, driving it through the back of the giant's head where it came to rest facing the Formorian army. One by one, Balor's soldiers died as the eye rested its gaze upon them.

David - ____________________

____

Goliath - ____________________

____

The metaphor - ____________________

____

Short Story Planner

DIRECTIONS: Fill in the information on the chart to help organize your ideas.

<u>Setting</u> When and where does the story take place? How will the setting affect the story?	
<u>Characters</u> Who are the people in your story? (Name and briefly describe each.) Who is David and who is Goliath? How will the reader know?	
<u>Plot</u> This is the conflict or obstacle the main character must overcome .	
<u>Beginning</u> How can you grab or "hook" the reader's attention? Introduce the setting, people, and possibly the plot here.	
<u>Middle</u> This is where you develop the story and build up the tension of the plot.	
<u>Resolution</u> How will the plot be resolved? What is the "rock" that helps the underdog in the story?	
<u>End</u> Here the conflict is resolved, though the story does NOT have to end happily.	

Short Story Scoring

Name ____________________

Story Title ____________________

0 – Unacceptable	2 – Fair	4 – Excellent
1 – Poor	3 – Good	

Category	**Student**	**Teacher**
Clear description of setting	______	______
Includes a clear metaphor	______	______
David and Goliath characters	______	______
Interesting introduction	______	______
Well-developed plot	______	______
Ending/plot resolution	______	______
Writing mechanics	______	______

Overall Score/Grade/Comments:

Short Story Scoring

Name ____________________

Story Title ____________________

0 – Unacceptable	2 – Fair	4 – Excellent
1 – Poor	3 – Good	

Category	**Student**	**Teacher**
Clear description of setting	______	______
Includes a clear metaphor	______	______
David and Goliath characters	______	______
Interesting introduction	______	______
Well-developed plot	______	______
Ending/plot resolution	______	______
Writing mechanics	______	______

Overall Score/Grade/Comments:

My Hero!

Springboard:

Students should complete "My Hero."

(Answers will of course vary, but should spark discussion.)

Objective: The student will be able to describe what typically happens in hero stories.

Materials:

My Hero (Springboard handout)
To Be a Hero... (handout)
King Arthur (handout)
Fitting the Mold? (handout)

Terms to know:

characteristics - defining qualities
initiation - going from one life stage to another
quest - search for something of great importance; can be spiritual or physical
supernatural - something that cannot be explained; magical
scapegoat - person or group that bears the blame for others

Procedure:

- Have student(s) complete the Springboard for around 3-5 minutes. Then have them share their ideas and discuss the characteristics of their heroes. Go on to explain that in this lesson the students will examine the characteristics of typical heroes in literature, poetry, and other writings.
- Distribute "To Be a Hero" and have the student(s) work independently or in pairs to read the characteristics and complete the exercise.
- Then, distribute "King Arthur" and "Fitting the Mold?" Have the student(s) read the handout and complete the graphic organizer. (Answers will vary but student(s) should use passage information to reason their answers)
- Go over the student(s)' ideas and discuss.

My Hero

DIRECTIONS: Free write for the assigned time in response to the following question (A free write is when you start writing and don't stop until time is called. Don't worry about grammar, spelling, or sentence structure. Just let your thoughts flow freely! A few ideas to get you started…

Who is your hero? Why? How do you know or know of him/her? What about him/her do you find "heroic"? What might you ask or say if you met your hero?

To Be A Hero...

DIRECTIONS: Read each of these characteristics that describe heroes in some writings. For each characteristic, provide at least one example of a character from books, movies or television that fits and then explain your answer.

Characteristic	Character Example	Explanation
Heroes sometimes have mystical or mysterious births.		
Heroes are often orphaned at a young age and raised by foster parents.		
Heroes are often unaware of their "real" identities until adolescence or adulthood.		
Heroes often live in seclusion and/or perform unusual feats as a child.		
Heroes sometimes undergo a trial or initiation as they moves from adolescence to adulthood.		
Heroes often undergo a quest to save a community or person.		
Heroes sometimes have friendly mentors or teachers who help with their quests.		
Heroes may have supernatural powers.		
Heroes are sometimes a scapegoat whose death is the only hope for a community.		

King Arthur

During the time of castles and kings, Prince Pendragon, the brother of King Uther was killed in battle during a terrible war between the Saxons and the Britons. Uther, bereft over his brother's death, called his chief advisor, Merlin, a longtime servant of the royal family. Now Merlin had special, magic powers, so Uther asked him to use his abilities to bring HUGE stones from Ireland and create a beautiful burial site for his beloved brother. This, Merlin did for his king, and today that site on the Salisbury Plain is known as Stonehenge.

Uther next asked Merlin to help form a Round Table, a group of knights from all over the land who would be bound by honor and a sacred oath to serve each other, the king, and their country. After the first meeting of the Round Table, a great festival was held in Carlisle, where Uther met the beautiful Igrain. He stared at her, entranced, but learned that she was already married to Gerlois, the Duke of Tintadiel. The couple, uncomfortable with the king's behavior, fled the festival. Uther, however, did not want to give up; so he declared Gerlois a rebel and sent his knights into Tintadiel to engage him in battle. As Gerlois was so engaged, Uther had time to charm Igrain. With Merlin's help, he transformed himself into a Gerlois look-alike and fooled Igrain into conceiving his child. When the real Gerlois was killed in battle, Uther married Igrain and she bore a son, Arthur.

After Arthur's birth, Merlin took the child as payment for all he had done for the king. Merlin sent Arthur to be raised by another knight, Sir Ector. Ector was a good and honorable man and raised Arthur as his own along with his real son, Sir Kay. The boys' childhood years were pleasant and free. Then when Arthur was fifteen, he and Sir Kay were out practicing their skills when Arthur saw a gleaming sword in a stone. Moving closer, he saw an inscription on it that read, "He whosoever draws forth this sword from the stone shall be the rightful king of England." And with that Arthur effortlessly pulled the sword out and so claimed the crown as the King of Briton.

This magical sword, called Excalibur, was very powerful and became a vital part of King Arthur's rule of Camelot, as he called his court filled with both followers and servants. In some stories it is said that the sparkling blade was so shiny, it blinded Arthur's enemies. There are other tales which tell of injuries from the sword that did not bleed. There are yet other sources that tell of the great sword being broken in a battle against King Pellinor and thrown in a lake, only to later be repaired and returned to Arthur by the Lady of the Lake.

In fact though tales about King Arthur vary, all report of great peace and harmony in Camelot, but achieved at a great cost. King Arthur had to use all of the powers of his sword to fight as many as twelve battles to bring peace to Briton. Both Excalibur and the magical Merlin supported the young king through the time of bloodshed. But after defeating many of his enemies, Arthur built a rich kingdom and court that would become the setting for many other Arthurian tales such as his love for Guinevere, the betrayal of Lancelot, the quest for the Holy Grail, and other long-told and fascinating stories.

Fitting the Mold?

DIRECTIONS: Use information from the "King Arthur" reading to complete the web.

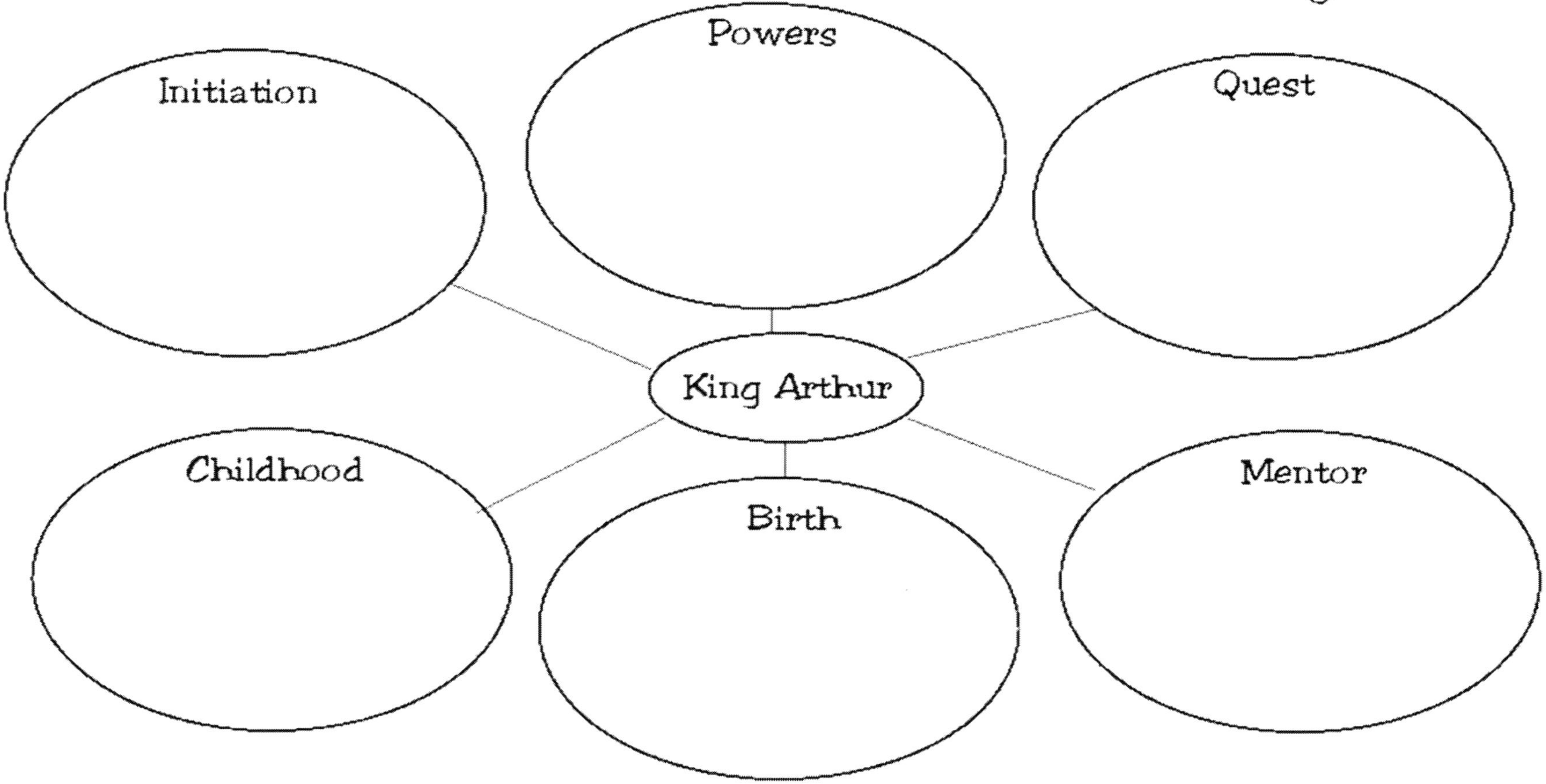

Do you think King Arthur qualifies as a hero, based on what you've learned. Why or why not? ____________________

____

____

____

____

Is It All a MYTHstake?

Springboard:

Students should complete "What Do You Know?"
(Answers may vary and include: robbed the rich to help the poor; had a band of Merry Men including Little John and Friar Tuck; was pursued by King John and the Sheriff of Nottingham; loved Maid Marion; won an archery contest, etc. Possible sources could be storybooks, movies, cartoons, etc.)

Objective: The student will be able to explain how legendary heroes are often based on the lives of real people.

Materials:
What Do You Know? (Springboard handout)
The Death of Robin Hood (handout)
Checking the Facts (handout)
The Real Robin Hood (handout)

Terms to know: **legend** - an exaggerated story based in part on historical facts

Procedure:

- While reviewing the Springboard, explain *that many legends, such as Robin Hood or King Arthur (from the previous lesson) are based on real people and experiences. Over time these stories become exaggerated and embellished to make them more exciting. In this lesson the student(s) will conduct research to learn the truth about Robin Hood.*
- Distribute "The Death of Robin Hood" and read the poem together. Explain that *the life and adventures of Robin Hood have been told over time, recited or sung in ballads and read in poetry* and have the student(s) explain what can be learned about Robin Hood from this short poem. (*2nd stanza – he lived in a forest; 4th stanza – was an archer; 7th stanza – lived outside the law, was brave*).

- Distribute "Checking the Facts." The student(s) should work independently or in pairs to select ten details about the life of Robin Hood from the lesson to research and either prove or disprove each. If the student(s) know little about him, a good site with legendary information is **www.boldoutlaw.com/**.
- Then they should write their own accounts of "The Real Robin Hood" based on their research. (*Answers will vary but note that the "true" stories are not as interesting as the legendary tales, which are often greatly exaggerated.*) Have the student(s) share their accounts and discuss.
- **EXTENSION:** Have the student(s) research another historical legend and report on what is fact and what is exaggerated. Possible topics include Lady Godiva, King Arthur, Beowulf, William Tell, Romulus and Remus, etc.

What Do You Know?

Brainstorm as many details as you can think of from the story of Robin Hood:

From what sources do you think you may have heard about Robin Hood? List as many as you can think of:

The Death of Robin Hood

By Bernard Barton (1784-1849)

His pulse was faint, his eye was dim.
And pale his brow of pride;
He heeded not the monkish hymn
They chanted by his side.

He knew his parting hour was come;
And fancy wandered now
To freedom's rude and lawless home,
Beneath the forest bough.

A faithful follower, standing by,
Asked where he would be laid;
Then round the chieftain's languid eye
A lingering lustre played.

"Now raise me on my dying bed,
Bring here my trusty bow,
And ere I join the silent dead,
My arm that spot shall show."

They raised him on his couch, and set
The casement open wide;
Once more with vain and fond regret
Fair Nature's face he eyed.

With kindling glance and throbbing heart
One parting look he case,
Sped on its way the feathered dart,
Sank back! And breathed his last!

And where it fell they dug his grave,
Beneath the greenwood tree;
Meet resting-place for one so brave,
So lawless, frank and free.

Checking the Facts

DIRECTIONS: Choose ten details from the story and use the Internet or other sources to check the validity of what you "know" about the life of Robin Hood.

Story Detail	True or False?	Supporting Evidence (facts)

The Real Robin Hood

DIRECTIONS: Use factual evidence to write a TRUE account of "Robin Hood."

ANSWER: Why do you think that your story is NOT the one most often told?

Have a Nice Trip!

Springboard:

Students should follow directions to complete "From Point A to Point B."

(Answers will vary, but students should recognize that people can encounter all kinds of problems and challenges on long journeys.)

Objective: The student will be able to describe characteristics of "journeys" that often occur in fiction and other literature.

Materials:

From Point A to Point B (Springboard handout)
Journey of a Lifetime (handout)
The Journey of Odysseus (3-page handout)

Terms to know:

journey - a trip taken by a character in the quest for treasure or to learn about himself/herself

trials and tribulations - painful experiences that test one's ability to carry on

Procedure:

- After reviewing the Springboard, explain that *in this lesson the student(s) will examine the theme of "journey" in fiction and other writings such as mythology*. Go on to explain that *the student(s) will consider what happens during such literary journeys*.
- Distribute "Journey of a Lifetime" and review the characteristics of journeys. Have the student(s) work independently or in pairs to generate examples of their own and share them.
- Distribute "The Journey of Odysseus" and explain that *Odysseus is the hero character from the famous Greek writer Homer's epic poem, the Odyssey.* Go on to explain that *although actually a long poem, Homer divided the Odyssey into 24 "books" of which the student(s) will read the 12 very "abridged" versions about the journey of Odysseus*. The student(s) should work individually or in pairs to read "Journey of a Lifetime," jotting notes in the space at right telling how this poem exemplifies a literary journey.
- Have the student(s) share and compare their ideas and discuss.

From Point A to Point B

DIRECTIONS: Pretend that you are planning a journey from the east coast to the west coast of the U.S. Choose any starting point on the eastern seaboard and draw a route west to any point on the western seaboard. Then, answer the questions below.

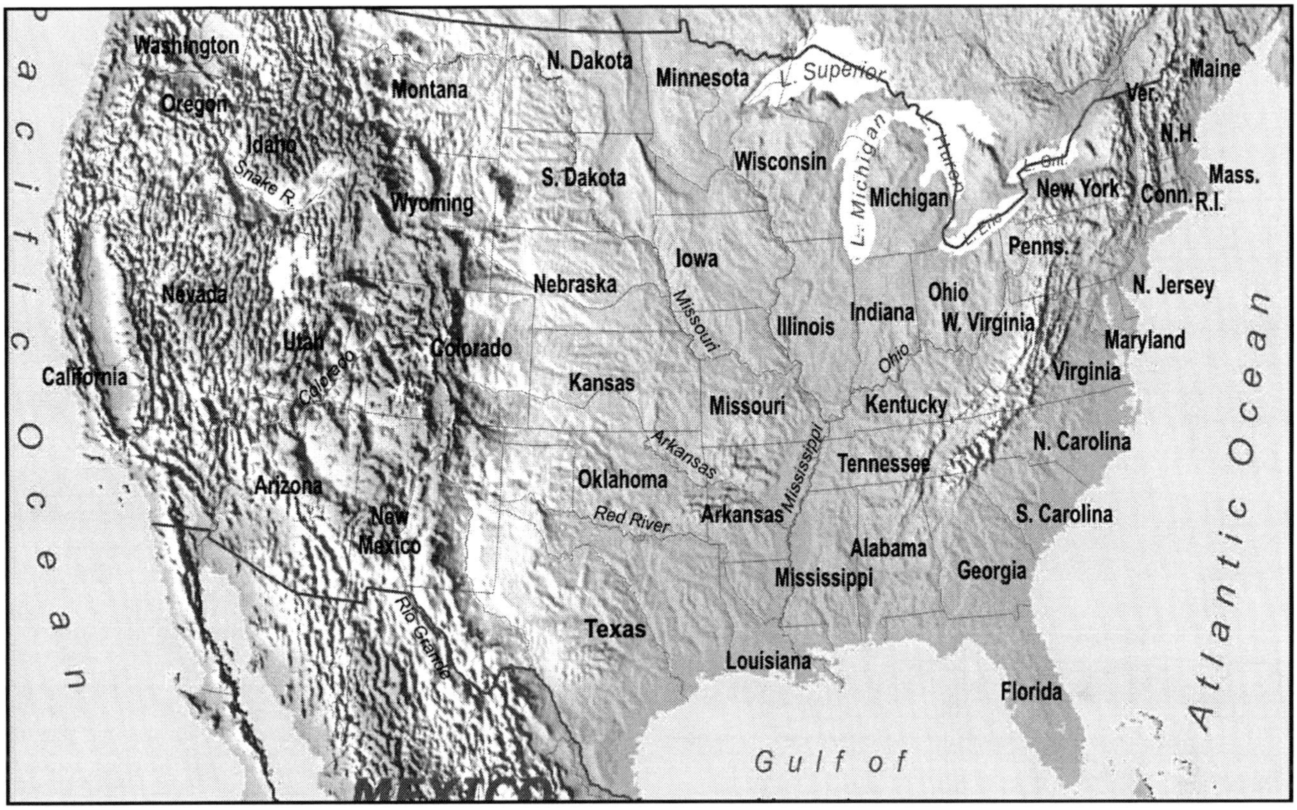

As you travel along your chosen route, what are some problems you might encounter?

____

____

____

____

____

How could you deal with those problems? ______________________

____

____

____

____

____

____

Journey of a Lifetime

DIRECTIONS: When a journey is part of non-realistic fiction (such as mythology, legends, etc.), the main character usually encounters one or more of the following situations. Read each and provide an example from a book, movie, or television show.

Fantastic places that exist nowhere in the real world: ____________________

____

____

____

____

Fantastic places with beautiful, enchanted landscapes: ____________________

____

____

____

____

Exciting and often life-threatening situations, such as battling dragons, giants, or other supernatural enemies: ____________________

____

____

____

____

Difficult terrains such as extremely high mountains or very deep seas: ______

____

____

____

____

Trials and tribulations that result in a new view on themselves, life, society, etc: ____________________

____

____

____

____

The Journey of Odysseus

Book One:
Homer begins his tale with a look at life among the gods of Mount Olympus. Athena, the goddess of war, convinces the others that the hero, Odysseus, has been marooned too long on the nymph's island of Calypso.

Book Two:
Meanwhile, back at Odysseus' home several men have tried to woo his wife, Penelope. They all think he's dead since he has been gone so long. His son, Telemachus, goes to the gods for help, and Zeus sends two eagles that tear out the throats of the suitors, killing them. Then, Telemachus heads out by sea to mainland Greece to try to find out what happened to his father.

Book Three:
Along the way Telemachus meets the 90-year-old King Nestor, who tells him that when the Greeks headed home after the Trojan War, they were separated. Some made it home safely, and some stayed behind to soothe Athena, the goddess of war, who was angry. He tells Telemachus to go to Egypt to see Menelaus, who might know where Odysseus is.

Book Four:
Menelaus did, in fact, have news of Odysseus because he and three other men had disguised themselves in sea animal skins and jumped on the Old Man of the Sea. They held him down until he told them what happened to their companions. According to the Old Man, Odysseus was being held against his will by the nymph Calypso.

Book Five:
Zeus sends his messenger, Hermes, on magic sandals over the waves to Calypso's island. Calypso is convinced to let Odysseus go, but the god Poseidon starts a storm with his spear and destroys Odysseus' raft. Odysseus barely escapes and washes to shore a few days later. He stumbles up the beach into an olive thicket and falls asleep.

The Journey of Odysseus

Book Six:
When he awakes, Odysseus hears women laughing and sees Princess Nausicaa of the Phaeacians and her maidens frolicking, washing her wedding dress in the river. Odysseus goes to the princess and begs her to help him get home. She kindly instructs him how to get the king's help, and he follows her into town.

Book Seven:
Odysseus is in awe of the beauty of the palace with its bronze walls and gemstone trim. Still he pleads with the king and queen to help him return home. The king agrees, but first invites the mysterious stranger to a feast.

Book Eight:
In honor of Odysseus the next day is declared a holiday. An athletic contest is held and Odysseus is invited to participate, but he declines. Some suggest that he does not join in because he is not athletic. Angered by the suggestion, Odysseus grabs a discus and throws it so hard that he frightens the people. That night he weeps as singers perform songs of the Trojan War. The king, who still does not know Odysseus's name, shouts "Enough! Our friend finds this song displeasing." He asks Odysseus, "Won't you please tell us your name, stranger, and where you are from?"

Book Nine:
Odysseus announces his name and that he is from Ithaca. He then goes on to tell the tale of how he lost many companions. Three of his crew, he explained, tasted the lotus-eater plant which made them lose all desire to go home. Then on another island, they found a cave full of goats herded by a Cyclops, a one-eyed monster that ate two of his men for dinner. A huge rock was put in place to keep them trapped. Since the Cyclops was so strong that only he had the strength to move the rock, the men couldn't kill him, so they gouged out his eye. While he groped around for them, they escaped by holding onto the undersides of the Cyclops' goats.

The Journey of Odysseus

Book Ten:
Odysseus and his men then met the Keeper of the Winds who tried to send them on their way with a good sailing breeze. However the Keeper had given Odysseus a bag, which his crew thought was treasure. When they opened the bag to see their gift, it released a hurricane that blew them back so they ended up fighting giants who threw huge boulders at their ships and ate some of the crew. The few survivors of that battle made it to the island of the nymph Circe, where they were enthralled with her enchanting ways. Unfortunately, she turned them all into pigs. Only Odysseus was protected by an herb he got from Hermes. Circe told him that to get home, he had to go through the land of Death.

Book Eleven:
The land of Death is filled with spirits with bodies that cannot talk. The only way to get them to talk, according to Circe, was to fill them with blood. According to her instructions, Odysseus sacrificed a lamb in a pit and fed the blood to the prophet Tiresias, who came back to life and told him how to get home.

Book Twelve:
On his way home, Odysseus met many other challenges. He had to pass the Sirens who lure sailors to their death with their singing. He used wax to plug his crews' ears to get past them. Then, he had to avoid Charybdis, a whirlpool that swallows up the sea. While steering away from Charybdis, they had to pass Scylla, a monster that grabbed six sailors with his horrible claws and gobbled them up. Finally, they made it to the island of Sun where what was left of his crew angered Zeus by killing his cattle. In a fury Zeus sent a thunderbolt to smash the ship, leaving only Odysseus who washed up on Calypso's shore.

The End of the Story...
After hearing his tale, the Phaeacians agree to get Odysseus home, disguised as a beggar. He reunites with his son and together, they plot to kill Penelope's suitors. Odysseus and his wife are reunited in the end, and Ithaca is at peace once more.

Growing Up

Springboard:
Students should study the 'To Kill a Mockingbird" plot summary and answer the question.
(Answers will vary. Given the limited information a student could justify the guilty verdict, the hypocrisy of Scout's teacher, or the attack at the end of the novel as turning points for Scout.)

Objective: The student will be able to describe the elements of coming of age stories.

Materials:
To Kill a Mockingbird (Springboard handout)
The Sniper (3-page handout)
Coming of Age Storyboard (handout)

Terms to know:
parapet - a low protective wall
civil war - fighting between people of the same country

Procedure:

- While reviewing the Springboard, explain that *To Kill a Mockingbird is one of the most famous and widely-read novels in American history. One of the major themes of the novel is the "coming of age" of the main character Scout Finch.*
- Distribute "The Sniper." Explain that *this story takes place in Dublin, Ireland at a time when a terrible civil war raged.* Have the student(s) read the story and answer the questions independently or in groups.
- Then have them share their answers and compare/contrast the reading with the Springboard story. (*Answers to the first question on the handout will vary. The second question should reflect an understanding that a traumatic event, a war, had forced the young sniper to grow up quickly. The killing of his brother at the end of the story would likely harden him even more. Comparisons and contrasts will vary.)*
- Hand out the "Coming of Age Storyboard." Explain that *an outline such as the one in the Springboard is just one way that an author can "map out" his or her story*. Go on to explain that *the student(s) will map out their own coming of age story using another approach, a storyboard format*. The student(s) should work individually or in groups to complete the assignment. **NOTE**: The storyboard assignment can be as simple or involved as desired, either to be finished in class or assigned for homework or a project.
- Have the student(s) share their storyboards and evaluate their work using the rubric provided.

TO KILL A MOCKINGBIRD

A PLOT SUMMARY

I. 1933-1934
   A. School starts (1st grade)
      1. Scout doesn't get along with her teacher Miss Caroline
      2. Boo Radley, the reclusive and strange neighbor, leaves gifts for Scout and her brother Jem
      3. Scout and Jem play the Boo Radley game, acting crazy, performing his mysterious history, and trying to spy on him
   B. Tom Robinson
      1. A black field hand
      2. Arrested for raping the 19-year-old daughter of the town drunk Bob Ewell
         a. Atticus (Scout's father) agrees to defend him in court
         b. Townspeople are angry at Atticus for defending a black man and Scout defends her father by fighting

II. 1935
   A. The lynch mob
      1. Group of men arrive at the courthouse to kill Tom
      2. Scout intervenes and unwittingly saves him when one of the men is shamed by her politeness
   B. The trial
      1. Atticus proves that Tom has been wrongly accused
      2. Scout and Jem hide in the balcony to watch the trial
      3. Jury finds Tom guilty
   C. After the trial
      1. Tom is shot 17 times when he attempts to escape prison
      2. Bob Ewell harasses and threatens Atticus, Tom's wife and the judge
      3. Scout questions the hypocrisy of her new teacher
      4. Jem never wants to speak of the trial again
      5. The school pageant
         a. Bob attacks Scout and Jem on their way home
         b. Boo Radley arrives and saves the children

At what point in the story do you think Scout "grew up," losing her childlike innocence? Explain your ideas.

The Sniper

By Liam O'Flaherty

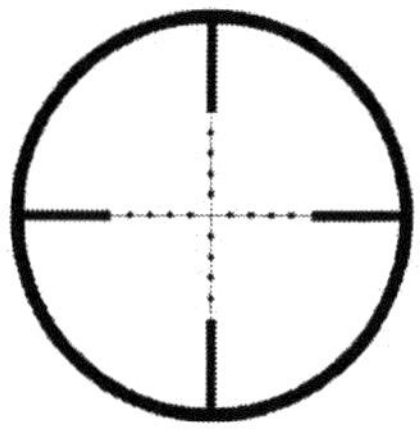

The long June twilight faded into night. Dublin lay enveloped in darkness but for the dim light of the moon that shone through fleecy clouds, casting a pale light as of approaching dawn over the streets and the dark waters of the Liffey. Around the beleaguered Four Courts, the heavy guns roared. Here and there through the city, machine guns and rifles broke the silence of the night, spasmodically, like dogs barking on lone farms. Republicans and Free Staters were waging civil war.

On a rooftop near O'Connell Bridge, a Republican sniper lay watching. Beside him lay his rifle and over his shoulders was slung a pair of field glasses. His face was the face of a student, thin and ascetic, but his eyes had the cold gleam of the fanatic. They were deep and thoughtful, the eyes of a man who is used to looking at death.

He was eating a sandwich hungrily. He had eaten nothing since morning. He had been too excited to eat. He finished the sandwich, and, taking a flask of whiskey from his pocket, he took a short draught. Then he returned the flask to his pocket. He paused for a moment, considering whether he should risk a smoke. It was dangerous. The flash might be seen in the darkness, and there were enemies watching. He decided to take the risk.

Placing a cigarette between his lips, he struck a match, inhaled the smoke hurriedly and put out the light. Almost immediately, a bullet flattened itself against the parapet of the roof. The sniper took another whiff and put out the cigarette. Then he swore softly and crawled away to the left.

Cautiously he raised himself and peered over the parapet. There was a flash and a bullet whizzed over his head. He dropped immediately. He had seen the flash. It came from the opposite side of the street.

He rolled over the roof to a chimney stack in the rear, and slowly drew himself up behind it until his eyes were level with the top of the parapet. There was nothing to be seen – just the dim outline of the opposite housetop against the blue sky. His enemy was under cover.

Just then an armored car came across the bridge and advanced slowly up the street. It stopped on the opposite side of the street, fifty yards ahead. The sniper could hear the dull panting of the motor. His heart beat faster. It was an enemy car. He wanted to fire, but he knew it was useless. His bullets would never pierce the steel that covered the gray monster.

Then round the corner of a side street came an old woman, her head covered by a tattered shawl. She began to talk to the man in the turret of the car. She was pointing to the roof where the sniper lay. An informer.

The turret opened. A man's head and shoulders appeared, looking toward the sniper. The sniper raised his rifle and fired. The head fell heavily on the turret wall. The woman darted toward the side street. The sniper fired again. The woman whirled round and fell with a shriek into the gutter.

Suddenly from the opposite roof a shot rang out and the sniper dropped his rifle with a curse. The rifle clattered to the roof. The sniper thought the noise would wake the dead. He stooped to pick the rifle up. He couldn't lift it. His forearm was dead. "I'm hit," he muttered.

Dropping flat onto the roof, he crawled back to the parapet. With his left hand he felt the injured right forearm. The blood was oozing through the sleeve of his coat. There was no pain – just a deadened sensation as if the arm had been cut off.

Quickly he drew his knife from his pocket, opened it on the breastwork of the parapet, and ripped open the sleeve. There was a small hole where the bullet had entered. On the other side there was no hole. The bullet had lodged in the bone. It must have fractured it. He bent the arm below the wound. The arm bent back easily. He ground his teeth to overcome the pain.

Then taking out his field dressing, he ripped open the packet with his knife. He broke the neck of the iodine bottle and let the bitter fluid drip into the wound. A paroxysm of pain swept through him. He placed the cotton wadding over the wound and wrapped the dressing over it. He tied the ends with his teeth.

Then he lay still against the parapet and, closing his eyes, he made an effort of will to overcome the pain.

In the street beneath, all was still. The armored car had retired speedily over the bridge with the machine gunner's head hanging lifeless over the turret. The woman's corpse lay still in the gutter.

The sniper lay still for a long time nursing his wounded arm and planning escape. Morning must not find him wounded on the roof. The enemy on the opposite roof covered his escape. He must kill that enemy and he could not use his rifle. He had only a revolver to do it. Then he thought of a plan.

Taking off his cap, he placed it over the muzzle of his rifle. Then he pushed the rifle slowly upward over the parapet, until the cap was visible from the opposite side of the street. Almost immediately there was a report, and a bullet pierced the center of the cap. The sniper slanted the rifle forward. The cap clipped down into the street. Then catching the rifle in the middle, the sniper dropped his left hand over the roof and let it hang, lifelessly. After a few moments he let the rifle drop to the street. Then he sank to the roof, dragging his hand with him.

Crawling quickly to his feet, he peered up at the corner of the roof. His ruse had succeeded. The other sniper, seeing the cap and rifle fall, thought that he had killed his man. He was now standing before a row of chimney pots, looking across with his head clearly silhouetted against the western sky.

The Republican sniper smiled and lifted his revolver above the edge of the parapet. The distance was about fifty yards – a hard shot in the dim light, and his right arm was paining him like a thousand devils. He took a steady aim. His hand trembled with eagerness. Pressing his lips together, he took a deep breath through his nostrils and fired. He was almost deafened with the report and his arm shook with the recoil.

Then when the smoke cleared, he peered across and uttered a cry of joy. His enemy had been hit. He was reeling over the parapet in his death agony. He struggled to keep his feet, but he was slowly falling forward as if in a dream. The rifle fell from his grasp, hit the parapet, fell over, bounded off the pole of a barber's shop beneath and then clattered on the pavement.

Then the dying man on the roof crumpled up and fell forward. The body turned over and over in space and hit the ground with a dull thud. Then it lay still.

The sniper looked at his enemy falling and he shuddered. The lust of battle died in him. He became bitten by remorse. The sweat stood out in beads on his forehead. Weakened by his wound and the long summer day of fasting and watching on the roof, he revolted from the sight of the shattered mass of his dead enemy. His teeth chattered, he began to gibber to himself, cursing the war, cursing himself, cursing everybody.

He looked at the smoking revolver in his hand, and with an oath he hurled it to the roof at his feet. The revolver went off with a concussion and the bullet whizzed past the sniper's head. He was frightened back to his senses by the shock. His nerves steadied. The cloud of fear scattered from his mind and he laughed.

Taking the whiskey flask from his pocket, he emptied it a draught. He felt reckless under the influence of the spirit. He decided to leave the roof now and look for his company commander to report. Everywhere around was quiet. There was not much danger in going through the streets. He picked up his revolver and put it in his pocket. Then he crawled down through the skylight to the house underneath.

When the sniper reached the laneway on the street level, he felt a sudden curiosity as to the identity of the enemy sniper whom he had killed. He decided that he was a good shot, whoever he was. He wondered did he know him. Perhaps he had been in his own company before the split in the army. He decided to risk going over to have a look at him. He peered around the corner into O'Connell Street. In the upper part of the street there was heavy firing, but around here all was quiet.

The sniper darted across the street. A machine gun tore up the ground around him with a hail of bullets, but he escaped. He threw himself face downward beside the corpse. The machine gun stopped.

Then the sniper turned over the dead body and looked into his brother's face.

What do you think the sniper was like prior to the civil war?_________________

____

____

____

____

____

____

Why could this be considered a coming of age story? Explain your ideas. ______

____

____

____

____

____

Coming of Age Storyboard

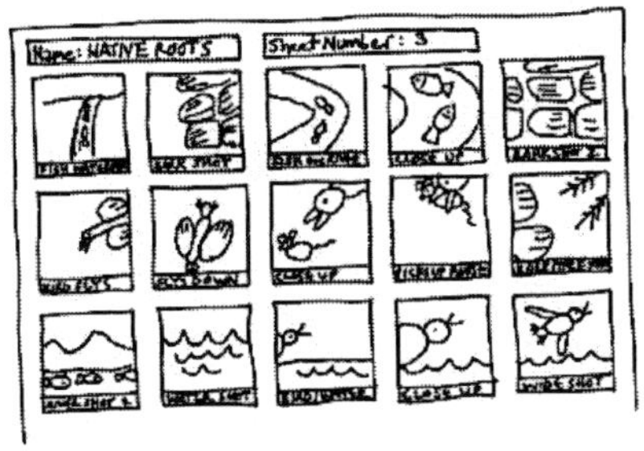

WHAT IS A STORYBOARD? A storyboard is a visual display of events. Storyboards are used to plan the order of events in movies, cartoons, and even home videos. The main events are drawn in "frames" or boxes much like a comic strip. Each frame shows the people, places, and key points to be made. Under each is a short written description of each event and notes may be included telling how they flow together.

THE ASSIGNMENT: In this lesson you will create a storyboard for an original coming of age story. The steps to complete it will be:

1. Decide on 6 - 8 events that your story will include.
2. Find or draw pictures to illustrate each event to create the "frames." These may be done on copy paper, poster board, etc.
3. Write short descriptions below each.
4. Make sure the events not only tell the action of the story, but also allow the reader to get to know the main character.
5. Evaluate your product and explanation using the rubric below.

Use the following scale to evaluate your work:

4 - Excellent   3 - Good   2 - Fair   1 - Poor   0 - Unacceptable

	Student Evaluation	**Teacher Evaluation**
Followed Assignment	_______	_______
Choice of Events (as explained)	_______	_______
Demonstrates knowledge of concept	_______	_______
Creative	_______	_______
Craftsmanship and Care	_______	_______

GRADE:

COMMENTS:

Wise Guys ... and Women

Springboard:

Students should read "Socrates" and answer the questions.

Objective: The student will be able to explain the importance of mentor characters in literature.

Materials:

Socrates (Springboard handout)
Supporting Characters (handout)
My Mentor (handout)
Letter-Writing (handout)

Terms to know:

mentor - someone who guides and advises a younger or less experienced person
philosopher - thinker
ethics - principles of right and wrong
protégé - someone who receives guidance and support from a mentor figure

Procedure:

- While reviewing the Springboard, review the definition of a "mentor" and discuss how Socrates fits the definition. Explain that *many works of literature including some already studied involve mentors.* Have the student(s) suggest some *(Merlin to King Arthur*, etc.) Go on to explain that *in this lesson the student(s) will study some famous literary mentors.*
- Distribute "Supporting Characters" and have the student(s) complete the exercise individually or in pairs. **NOTE**: The student(s) can briefly research one of the characters if they are not familiar with any of them.
- Share, compare, and discuss the importance of these characters in their corresponding stories.
- Now explain that *the student(s) are going to think about people in their own lives who have served as mentors and write a letter to thank one that stands out*.
- Distribute "My Mentor" and have the student(s) complete the brainstorming exercise using the graphic organizer.
- Then hand out the "Letter Writing" and review the correct format. Have the student(s) write their letters.
- Have them share the letter, if desired, and discuss what mentors often have in common (*gifts and knowledge for the protégé, an unselfish desire to help, etc.).*

Socrates

Socrates is known as one of the greatest philosophers of all time. He lived in ancient Athens, a city-state in Greece, from 469 B.C. to 399 B.C. His life was spent seeking truth and asking those around him to examine their own thoughts and evaluate their beliefs and motives. To do this, he asked people a series of questions to provoke conversations on a variety of topics.

Socrates was in fact one of the most famous teachers in history. He had no dry erase board, no Internet, nor textbooks; yet his teachings and his approach live on today. He encouraged his students to think for themselves and used his "Socratic method" to encourage them to draw their own conclusions and support their ideas. One of his students, Plato, became famous in his own right, using the knowledge he gained from Socrates in his written dialogues and the first book ever written on political science, called *The Republic*. Plato then taught another famous Greek, Aristotle, who shared what he learned with his own students at the Lyceum, a school in Athens. Aristotle had famous pupils as well, most notably, Alexander the Great.

Since Socrates was rather **unconventional** for his time, he often got in trouble with the Athenian government. By questioning accepted Greek beliefs about religion, ethics, and politics, he was brought to trial for corrupting the youth of Athens and teaching "false religion." After being sentenced to death in 399 B.C., he could easily have escaped with the help of his students. However, as much as Socrates encouraged people to question society, he still believed all citizens should obey the law, so he refused to flee. He died after drinking poison made from the hemlock plant, leaving his students to mourn his death.

The word **unconventional** in the last paragraph **MOST NEARLY** means

A. traditional.
B. unusual.
C. common.
D. popular.

The most important teaching tool Socrates used was

A. encouraging lawlessness.
B. textbooks and dialogue.
C. asking questions.
D. oral examinations.

Which of these sentences states a correct relationship?

A. Socrates was Aristotle's mentor.
B. Aristotle was a protégé of Plato's.
C. Socrates taught Alexander the Great.
D. Alexander was Plato's favorite student.

Do you think Socrates a good mentor? Why or why not? ____________________

____

____

____

____

Socrates - Answers and Explanations

Socrates is known as one of the greatest philosophers of all time. He lived in ancient Athens, a city-state in Greece, from 469 B.C. to 399 B.C. His life was spent seeking truth and asking those around him to examine their own thoughts and evaluate their beliefs and motives. To do this, he asked people a series of questions to provoke conversations on a variety of topics.

Socrates was in fact one of the most famous teachers in history. He had no dry erase board, no Internet, nor textbooks; yet his teachings and his approach live on today. He encouraged his students to think for themselves and used his "Socratic method" to encourage them to draw their own conclusions and support their ideas. One of his students, Plato, became famous in his own right, using the knowledge he gained from Socrates in his written dialogues and the first book ever written on political science, called *The Republic*. Plato then taught another famous Greek, Aristotle, who shared what he learned with his own students at the Lyceum, a school in Athens. Aristotle had famous pupils as well, most notably, Alexander the Great.

Since Socrates was rather **unconventional** for his time, he often got in trouble with the Athenian government. By questioning accepted Greek beliefs about religion, ethics, and politics, he was brought to trial for corrupting the youth of Athens and teaching "false religion." After being sentenced to death in 399 B.C., he could easily have escaped with the help of his students. However, as much as Socrates encouraged people to question society, he still believed all citizens should obey the law, so he refused to flee. He died after drinking poison made from the hemlock plant, leaving his students to mourn his death.

The word **unconventional** in the last paragraph **MOST NEARLY** means

A. traditional.
B. unusual. *
C. common.
D. popular.

(The passage states that he questioned "accepted" beliefs, indicating he was unlike most others of the day.)

The most important teaching tool Socrates used was

A. encouraging lawlessness.
B. textbooks and dialogue.
C. asking questions. *
D. oral examinations.

(The passage discussed his Socratic method, which involved asking questions to make his students draw and defend their own conclusions.)

Which of these sentences states a correct relationship?

A. Socrates was Aristotle's mentor.
B. Aristotle was a protégé of Plato's. *
C. Socrates taught Alexander the Great.
D. Alexander was Plato's favorite student.

(Though students may not yet know the meaning of the word "protégé," the other choices are definitely false.)

Was Socrates a good mentor? Why or why not?

Answers will vary but should demonstrate an understanding of the term "mentor."

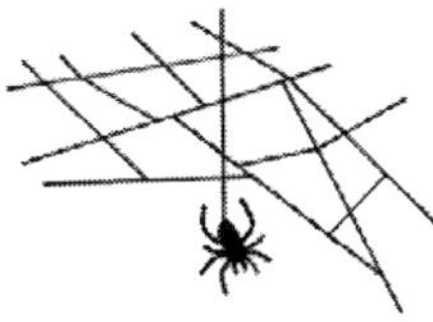

"Supporting" Characters

Choose one of these characters and complete the analysis below:

Obi-Wan Kenobi	Charlotte (from Charlotte's Web)
Yoda	Owl (from Winnie the Pooh)
Albus Dumbledore	Glenda the Good Witch
The Fairy Godmother	Gandalf

Who was the protégé in the story? How did the mentor help him/her?

What gifts or powers did the mentor possess? How did these and other characteristics make him/her a good mentor?

Why do you think the character served as a mentor? What was "in it" for him/her?

How do you think the story would have been different if the mentor did not exist?

How did the mentor make the story more interesting?

My Mentor...

This Person's "Gifts" to You

Quote Describing the Person

Name and Relationship to You

Person's Special Qualities

How You Might "Pass On" What You've Learned from this Person

Letter Writing

DIRECTIONS: Write a letter to your mentor, thanking him or her for the positive impact on your life. Use your notes and quotes from the mentor diagram. Make sure you include:

- a proper salutation ("Dear ...")
- an opening paragraph that describes the purpose of your letter
- a body paragraph that includes details
- a closing paragraph that explains how this person affects your future plans
- a signature line and signature

Literary Ladies

Springboard:
Students should read "Cleopatra" and answer the question.
(Answers may vary, but should be based on passage information.)

Objective: The student will be able to describe some common female archetypes in literature.

Materials:
Cleopatra (Springboard handout)
It's a Girl! (handout)
What a Woman! (handout or transparency)

Terms to know:
archetype - typical example, model
seductress - woman who lures, tempts others
nurture - to take care of, to encourage

Procedure:

- After reviewing the Springboard explain that *Cleopatra represents many female archetypes (review term) prevalent in literature: the seductress because she married Caesar even though he was already married; the boss because she was a pharaoh; the murderess since she killed her brother; the nurturer for her several children, etc.* Go on to explain *that in this lesson the student(s) will examine several female archetypes that appear often in literature*.
- Distribute "It's a Girl!" and have the student(s) work independently, in pairs, or small groups to predict a description of each archetype, taking into account what each character would be like in a story. For now, the student(s) should leave the "Character Example" and "Character Explanation" columns blank.
- Have the student(s) share and compare their descriptions to the teacher answer page.

- Then display or hand out "What a Woman!" The student(s) should work on their own or with their partner or group to briefly research each character as needed and complete the blank columns on their handouts.
- Encourage student(s) to add their own examples to the chart in addition to those provided.
- Have the student(s) share and compare their responses and discuss.

Cleopatra - Queen of the Nile

Cleopatra was born in 69 B.C. into the royal family of Egypt. Her father, Ptolemy XII, died in 51 B.C. and upon his death declared that she and her twelve-year-old brother would marry and rule the land together. Though largely Greek by blood, her family had long ruled Egypt. Cleopatra herself dearly loved Egypt and was popular among the Egyptians. The people viewed her as one of them and accepted her as pharaoh. However, she was not very popular among the military. Since they could not control her as they would have liked, the generals forced her from power in 48 B.C. and made her brother sole ruler.

Cleopatra looked to the fifty-four-year-old Roman general Julius Caesar to return her rule. Caesar arrived in Egypt with an army far larger than the Egyptians' and she plotted to get the Romans' support. She had an expensive rug delivered to Caesar as a gift. When he unrolled it, he found the beautiful twenty-two-year-old Cleopatra inside. The two "fell in love" and Caesar used his army to capture and kill those that had forced her from power, including her brother who drowned in the Nile River fleeing for his life.

The couple spent the next several months sailing the Nile, where Caesar saw firsthand how the Egyptian people worshipped Cleopatra. Although he knew he would never be accepted as a pharaoh, he thought a marriage between them might unite his empire and hers.

In 46 B.C. the pair returned to Rome, home to the wife Caesar had left behind, with their new son, Caesarion. This, along with a general Roman distrust of foreigners, made Cleopatra very unpopular. Over the next two years, Caesar became dictator of Rome, made many changes, and remained popular with the people. Yet he also had many rivals who resented his power; they plotted against him and carried out his murder in 44 B.C. Fearing for her life without Caesar's protection, Cleopatra fled to Egypt, murdered her second brother, and named her four-year-old son Egypt's new king.

DIRECTIONS: List as many adjectives as you can think of to describe Cleopatra:

______________	______________	______________
______________	______________	______________
______________	______________	______________
______________	______________	______________
______________	______________	______________
______________	______________	______________
______________	______________	______________
______________	______________	______________

It's a Girl!

Archetype	Description	Character	Explanation
The Boss			
The Seductress			
The Spunky Kid			
The Free Spirit			
The Waif			
The Librarian			

It's a Girl! - Suggestions for Answers

Archetype	Description	Character	Explanation
The Boss	*Goal oriented, take charge, in control, decision maker*	*Answers will vary*	*Answers will vary, but should be well-reasoned.*
The Seductress	*Manipulative, survivor, beautiful, uses looks to get her way*	*Answers will vary.*	*Answers will vary, but should be well-reasoned*
The Spunky Kid	*Girl next door, team player, full of energy, tom-boy, quick witted and likable*	*Answers will vary.*	*Answers will vary, but should be well-reasoned*
The Free Spirit	*Optimistic, follows her heart, takes chances to find happiness*	*Answers will vary.*	*Answers will vary, but should be well-reasoned*
The Waif	*Damsel in distress, endures hardships, needs male support*	*Answers will vary.*	*Answers will vary, but should be well-reasoned*
The Librarian	*Prim and proper, repressed, strict, follows the rules*	*Answers will vary.*	*Answers will vary, but should be well-reasoned*

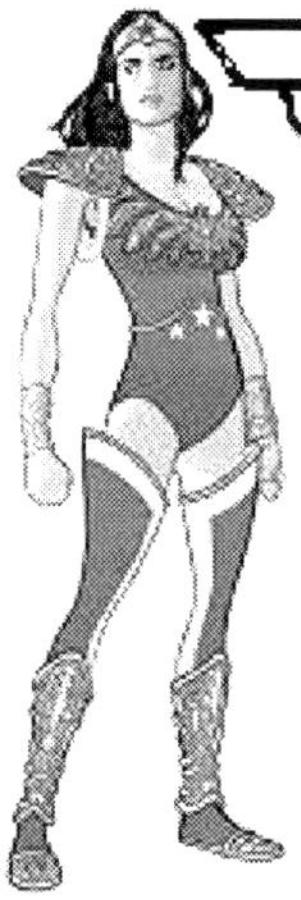

What a Woman!

DIRECTIONS: Briefly research each of the following female characters to decide which archetype they represent. Then, fill in the names on the "It's a Girl!" chart and explain your answers.

Scarlett O'Hara -

Nancy Drew -

Little Orphan Annie -

Jane Eyre -

Marge Simpson -

Joan of Arc -

Melanie Wilkes -

Ellen Ripley -

Princess Buttercup -

Auntie Mame -

Mary Poppins -

Hermione Granger -

Laura Ingalls -

Guinevere -

Ariel the Little Mermaid -

Lady Macbeth -

Pippi Longstocking -

He Loves Me; He Loves Me Not

Springboard:

Students should read "Two Star-Crossed Lovers" and answer the questions.

Objective: Students will recognize the universal theme of the star-crossed lovers throughout literary history.

Materials:
Two Star-Crossed Lovers (Springboard handout)
Teenage Drama (handout)
It's Only the Beginning (handout)

Terms to know:
prologue - an introduction to a poem, story, play, or other literary work (sometimes in verse)
star-crossed lovers - a forbidden romance theme in literature

Procedures:

- After reviewing the Springboard, explain that *this lesson further examines the star-crossed lovers theme.*
- Distribute the "Teenage Drama" handout and review the directions. Then have the student(s) work individually, in pairs, or small groups to answer the questions based on any book, play, movie, etc. they can think of in which the star-crossed lover theme plays out.
- Have them share their answers, hand out the "It's Only the Beginning" page, and review. The student(s) should then work individually or in pairs to write a prologue to the story, book, movie, etc.
- Have them share their writings, evaluate their work, and discuss, including the following questions:
  - ? In what way(s) are all the star-crossed lover stories similar? *(Two young people from different backgrounds, warring tribes or groups, species, etc. fall in love against all odds, but cannot be together. Thus the tale ends unhappily.)*
  - ? What decisions do the characters in the story make, and how do these decisions lead to tragedy? *(Answers will vary with the story.)*
  - ? How do other characters react to the tragedy? What, if any, lessons are learned? *(Answers may vary.)*

Two Star-Crossed Lovers

You've seen or read it before: two young people, usually teens, in love, but caught in a situation that keep them apart. Wars, fate, family or gang feuds, species; or even something as simple as a few hundred miles keeps the lovelorn apart. In many cases one or both of the characters dies, leaving the reader or viewer teary-eyed, hoping the two will once more be together, if only in death.

The most famous example of this theme or archetype is Shakespeare's *Romeo and Juliet*, though similar stories have been around since ancient times. Some tell of lovers separated by different stations in life, warring countries or tribes, religious, racial, or other differences. In some, one of the characters may be leaving or dying. Whatever the reasons for the separation, the effect is the same - utter and total tragedy! Lives lost, families torn apart, futures destroyed, pasts blurred such that those left behind can only grieve and wonder, "How could this have happened?"

Romeo and Juliet
by William Shakespeare
ACT I: PROLOGUE

Two households, both alike in dignity,
In fair Verona, where we lay our scene,
From ancient grudge break to new mutiny,
Where civil blood makes civil hands unclean.
From forth the fatal loins of these two foes
A pair of star-cross'd lovers take their life;
Whole misadventured piteous overthrows
Do with their death bury their parents' strife.
The fearful passage of their death-mark'd love,
And the continuance of their parents' rage,
Which, but their children's end, nought could remove,
Is now the two hours' traffic of our stage;
That which if you with patient ears attend,
What here shall miss, our toil shall strive to mend.

Based on the story's prologue, Shakespeare's *Romeo and Juliet* is an EXCELLENT example of a star-crossed lovers' tale because

A. the couple in the story has many misadventures.
B. a death leads two groups to mend their differences.
C. the prologue uses the words "star-cross'd lovers."
D. an ancient grudge leads two lovers to take their lives.

Based on the example from *Romeo and Juliet*, it can be concluded that a "prologue"

A. tells of death and misadventures.
B. comes at the beginning of a story.
C. introduces the characters in a play.
D. is a writing by William Shakespeare.

A reader can expect star-crossed lovers in a story to end

A. happily ever after.
B. with a big wedding.
C. sorrowfully.
D. mysteriously.

Two Star-Crossed Lovers - Answers and Explanations

You've seen or read it before: two young people, usually teens, in love, but caught in a situation that keep them apart. Wars, fate, family or gang feuds, species; or even something as simple as a few hundred miles keeps the lovelorn apart. In many cases one or both of the characters dies, leaving the reader or viewer teary-eyed, hoping the two will once more be together, if only in death.

The most famous example of this theme or archetype is Shakespeare's *Romeo and Juliet*, though similar stories have been around since ancient times. Some tell of lovers separated by different stations in life, warring countries or tribes, religious, racial, or other differences. In some, one of the characters may be leaving or dying. Whatever the reasons for the separation, the effect is the same - utter and total tragedy! Lives lost, families torn apart, futures destroyed, pasts blurred such that those left behind can only grieve and wonder, "How could this have happened?"

Romeo and Juliet

by William Shakespeare

ACT I: <u>PROLOGUE</u>

Two households, both alike in dignity,
In fair Verona, where we lay our scene,
From ancient grudge break to new mutiny,
Where civil blood makes civil hands unclean.
From forth the fatal loins of these two foes
A pair of star-cross'd lovers take their life;
Whole misadventured piteous overthrows
Do with their death bury their parents' strife.
The fearful passage of their death-mark'd love,
And the continuance of their parents' rage,
Which, but their children's end, nought could remove,
Is now the two hours' traffic of our stage;
That which if you with patient ears attend,
What here shall miss, our toil shall strive to mend.

Based on the story's prologue, Shakespeare's *Romeo and Juliet* is an <u>EXCELLENT</u> example of a star-crossed lovers' tale because

A. the couple in the story has many misadventures.
B. a death leads two groups to mend their differences.
C. the prologue uses the words "star-cross'd lovers."
D. an ancient grudge leads two lovers to take their lives. *

(Though A and B are true, they don't define the genre; and C doesn't make sense.)

Based on the example from *Romeo and Juliet*, it can be concluded that a "prologue"

A. tells of death and misadventures.
B. comes at the beginning of a story. *
C. introduces the characters in a play.
D. is a writing by William Shakespeare.

(The fact that it is "Act I" implies it is at the beginning of the story.)

A reader can expect star-crossed lovers in a story to end

A. happily ever after.
B. with a big wedding.
C. sorrowfully. *
D. mysteriously.

(Since the tale involves death, tragedy, and grief, C is the best choice.)

Teenage Drama

DIRECTIONS: Think of a book, movie, play, etc. about star-crossed lovers, and answer these questions based on what you read or saw.

TITLE - ____________________

LITERARY FORM - ____________________

Who are the star-crossed lovers in the story, and what keeps them apart? ______

How does the couple fall in love, and who knows/doesn't know about their love?

Explain the tragedy that befalls the young people. ____________________

Who is "left behind," and how do the characters cope with the tragedy? ________

It's Only the Beginning

DIRECTIONS: Use information from your "Teenage Drama" answers to write a "prologue" for the book, movie, play, etc. you analyzed. It can be in prose (paragraph form) or verse (poetic), but should give a brief overview of the story and pique the reader's or viewer's interest.

____

____

____

____

____

____

____

____

____

____

____

____

____

____

____

____

____

____

Star-Crossed Rubric

Title ______________________________ **Form** ____________

4 – excellent
3 – good
2 – fair
1 – poor
0 – unacceptable

	Self-evaluation
Selection represents theme	_____
Summarizes story	_____
Creativity of presentation	_____
Spelling, grammar, form	_____

Grade:

Comments:

It's Inhuman!

Springboard:
Students should complete "The Golden Rule."
(Answers will vary but should spark discussion.)

Objective: The student will be able to recognize and describe the theme of inhumanity in literature and other works.

Materials:
The Golden Rule (Springboard handout)
Andrew Jackson on Indian Removal (2-page handout)
Chief Seattle's 1854 Oration (handout)
Breaking it Down (handout)
Putting It into Words (handout)

Terms to know: **inhumanity** - terrible treatment of another person

Procedure:

- After reviewing the Springboard, explain that *many books, movies, and plays portray the opposite of the golden rule - the horrible treatment of man against others.* Go on to explain that *in this lesson the student(s) will analyze another form of writing, speeches, to examine this theme.*
- **For group instruction** have students work in pairs, each reading a speech and filling out the corresponding half of "Breaking it Down." Then have them share their half of the analysis with their partner so that he/she can fill in the other half of their form.
- **For individual instruction** the student should read both speeches to complete the form.
- Have students share their answers and lead a discussion of other examples of the theme (*any work about the Holocaust, slavery, war, terrorism, etc.)*.
- Distribute "Putting It into Words" and have the student(s) write a poem as directed to express the native peoples' feelings about removal and the U.S. government.
- Have the student(s) share their creations.

The Golden Rule

"Do unto others as you would have them do unto you."

Examples of following the golden rule	Examples of NOT following the golden rule

Why do you think this saying is called the "golden rule?" ____________

____

____

____

There are versions of the golden rule in all religions, languages and cultures. Why do you think this is so? ______________________

____

____

____

What does the golden rule mean to you? Restate it in your own words.

____

____

____

Why do you think some people don't follow this rule? ____________

____

____

____

ANDREW JACKSON ON INDIAN REMOVAL (1830)

"It gives me pleasure to announce to Congress that the … policy of the Government, steadily pursued for nearly thirty years, in relation to the removal of the Indians beyond the white settlements is approaching to a happy consummation. Two important tribes have accepted the provision made for their removal at the last session of Congress, and it is believed that their example will induce the remaining tribes also to seek the same obvious advantages.

The consequences of a speedy removal will be important to the United States, to individual States, and to the Indians themselves. The (financial) advantages which it Promises to the Government are the least of its recommendations. It puts an end to all possible danger of collision between the authorities of the General and State Governments on account of the Indians. It will place a dense and civilized population in large tracts of country now occupied by a few savage hunters. By opening the whole territory between Tennessee on the north and Louisiana on the south to the settlement of the whites it will … strengthen the southwestern frontier and render the adjacent States strong enough to repel future invasions without remote aid. It will relieve the whole State of Mississippi and the western part of Alabama of Indian occupancy, and enable those States to advance rapidly in population, wealth, and power. It will separate the Indians from immediate contact with settlements of whites; free them from the power of the States; enable them to pursue happiness in their own way and under their own rude institutions; will retard the progress of decay which is lessening their numbers, and perhaps cause them gradually, under the protection of the Government and through the influence of good counsels, to cast off their savage habits and become an interesting, civilized, and Christian community. …

With a full understanding of the subject, the Choctaw and the Chickasaw tribes have (agreed to the generous) offers presented by the Act of Congress, and have agreed to remove beyond the Mississippi River. Treaties have been made with them, which in due season will be submitted for consideration. In negotiating these treaties they were made to understand their true condition, and they have preferred maintaining their independence in the Western forests to submitting to the laws of the States in which they now reside. These treaties, being probably the last which will ever be made with them, are characterized by great liberality on the part of the Government. They give the Indians a liberal sum in consideration of their removal, and comfortable subsistence on their arrival at their new homes.....

Nor is there anything in this which, upon a comprehensive view of the general interests of the human race, is to be regretted. Philanthropy could not wish to see this continent restored to the conditions in which it was found by our forefathers. What good man would prefer a country covered with forests and ranged by a few thousand savages to our extensive Republic, studded with cities, towns, and prosperous farms, embellished with all the improvements which art can devise or industry execute, occupied by more than 12,000,000 happy people, and filled with all the blessings of liberty, civilization, and religion?

The present policy of the Government is but a continuation of the same progressive change by a milder process. The tribes which occupied the countries now constituting the Eastern States were annihilated or have melted away to make room for the whites. The waves of population and civilization are rolling to the westward, and we now propose to acquire the countries occupied by the red men of the South and West by a fair exchange, and, at the expense of the United States, to send them to a land where their existence may be prolonged and perhaps made perpetual. Doubtless it will be painful to leave the graves of their fathers; but what do they more than our ancestors did or than our children are now doing? To better their condition in an unknown land our forefathers left all that was dear in earthly objects. Our children by thousands yearly leave the land of their birth to seek new homes in distant regions. Does Humanity weep at these painful separations from everything, animate and inanimate, with which the young heart has become entwined? Far from it. ....Can it be cruel in this Government when, by events which it can not control, the Indian is made discontented in his ancient home to purchase his lands, to give him a new and extensive territory, to pay the expense of his removal, and support him a year in his new abode? How many thousands of our own people would gladly embrace the opportunity of removing to the West on such conditions! If the offers made to the Indians were extended to them, they would be hailed with gratitude and joy.

And is it supposed that the wandering savage has a stronger attachment to his home than the settled, civilized Christian? Is it more afflicting to him to leave the graves of his fathers than it is to our brothers and children? Rightly considered, the policy of the General Government toward the red man is not only liberal, but generous. He is unwilling to submit to the laws of the States and mingle with their population. To save him from this alternative, or perhaps utter annihilation, the General Government kindly offers him a new home, and proposes to pay the whole expense of his removal and settlement..."

CHIEF SEATTLE (1854)

"Yonder sky that has wept tears of compassion upon my people for centuries untold, and which to us appears changeless and eternal, may change. Today is fair. Tomorrow it may be overcast with clouds. My words are like the stars that never change. Whatever Seattle says, the great chief at Washington can rely upon with as much certainty as he can upon the return of the sun or the seasons. The white chief says that Big Chief at Washington sends us greetings of friendship and goodwill. This is kind of him for we know he has little need of our friendship in return. His people are many. They are like the grass that covers vast prairies. My people are few. They resemble the scattering trees of a storm-swept plain. The great - and I presume good - White Chief sends us word that he wishes to buy our land but is willing to allow us enough to live comfortably. This indeed appears just, even generous, for the Red Man ... as we are no longer in need of an extensive country.

There was a time when our people covered the land as the waves of a wind-ruffled sea cover its shell-paved floor, but that time long since passed away with the greatness of tribes that are now but a mournful memory. I will not dwell on, nor mourn over, our untimely decay, nor reproach my paleface brothers with hastening it, as we too may have been somewhat to blame.

Youth is impulsive. When our young men grow angry at some real or imaginary wrong, and disfigure their faces with black paint, it denotes that their hearts are black, and that they are often cruel ... and our old men and old women are unable to restrain them... Thus it was when the white man began to push our forefathers ever westward. But let us hope that the hostilities between us may never return. We would have everything to lose and nothing to gain...

Our good father in Washington... sends us word that if we do as he desires he will protect us. His brave warriors will be to us a bristling wall of strength, and his wonderful ships of war will fill our harbors so that our ancient enemies far to the northward (Canadian tribes) will cease to frighten our women, children, and old men. Then in reality he will be our father and we his children. But can that ever be? Your God is not our God! Your God loves your people and hates mine! He folds his strong protecting arms lovingly about the paleface and leads him by the hand as a father leads an infant son. But He has forsaken His Red children, if they really are His. Our God, the Great Spirit, seems also to have forsaken us. Your God makes your people wax stronger every day. Soon they will fill all the land. Our people are ebbing away like a rapidly receding tide that will never return. The white man's God cannot love our people or He would protect them. They seem to be orphans who can look nowhere for help. How then can we be brothers? How can your God become our God and renew our prosperity and awaken in us dreams of returning greatness? If we have a common Heavenly Father He must be partial, for He came to His paleface children. We never saw Him. He gave you laws but had no word for His red children whose teeming multitudes once filled this vast continent as stars fill the firmament. No; we are two distinct races with separate origins and separate destinies. There is little in common between us…

Day and night cannot dwell together. The Red Man has ever fled the approach of the White Man as the morning mist flees before the morning sun. However, your proposition seems fair and I think that my people will accept it and will retire to the reservation you offer them. Then we will dwell apart in peace, for the words of the Great White Chief seem to be the words of nature speaking to my people out of dense darkness.

It matters little where we pass the remnant of our days. They will not be many. The Indian's night promises to be dark. Not a single star of hope hovers above his horizon. Sad-voiced winds moan in the distance. Grim fate seems to be on the Red Man's trail, and wherever he will hear the approaching footsteps of his destroyer and prepare stolidly to meet his doom, as does the wounded doe that hears the approaching footsteps of the hunter.

A few more moons, a few more winters, and not one of the descendants of the mighty hosts that once moved over this broad land or lived in happy homes protected by the Great Spirit will remain to mourn over the graves of a people once more powerful and hopeful than yours. But why should I mourn at the untimely fate of my people? Tribe follows tribe, and nation follows nation, like the waves of the sea. It is the order of nature, and regret is useless. Your time of decay may be distant but it will surely come, for even the White Man whose God walked and talked with him as friend to friend, cannot be exempt from the common destiny. We may be brothers after all. We will see…

And when the last Red Man shall have perished and the memory of my tribe shall have become a myth among the White Men, these shores will swarm with the invisible dead of my tribe, and when your children's children think themselves alone in the field, the store, the shop, upon the highway, or in the silence of the pathless woods, they will not be alone. In all the earth there is no place dedicated to solitude. At night when the streets of your cities and villages are silent and you think them deserted, they will throng with the returning hosts that once filled them and still love this beautiful land. The White Man will never be alone… Let him be just and deal kindly with my people, for the dead are not powerless. Dead, did I say? There is no death, only a change of worlds."

B-R-E-A-K-I-N-G IT DOWN

ANDREW JACKSON		CHIEF SEATTLE
	PURPOSE	
	AUDIENCE	
	USE OF LANGUAGE	
	TONE	
	OVERALL IMPACT	

Putting It Into Words

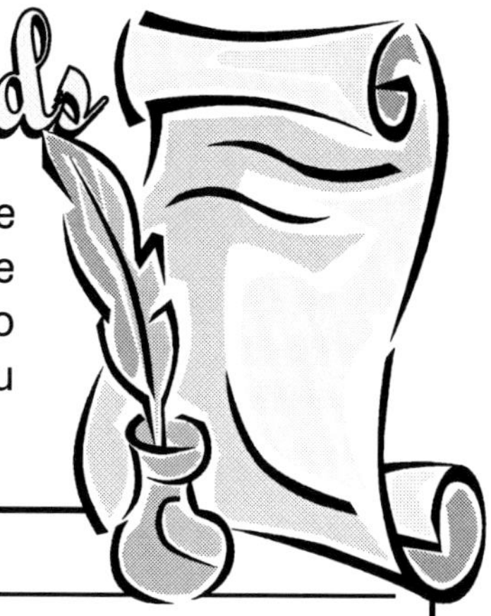

DIRECTIONS: Write a poem to express what you think Native Americans would have felt about removal and the way they were treated by other humans. It can rhyme or be free verse with no particular rhythm or format. Make sure you include a title. You can also use illustrations to enhance the meaning of your words.

A Perfect World?

Springboard:
Students should complete the "In a Perfect World..." handout, brainstorming descriptions for each category.
(Answers will vary.)

Objective: The student will be able to describe the idea of utopia in literature.

Materials:
In a Perfect World... (Springboard handout)
Harrison Bergeron (4-page handout)
R U 4 Real? (handout)

Terms to know:
utopia - a perfect society in which all citizens lead a blissful life
dystopia - a society which is depressingly horrible and whose citizens lead fearful and wretched lives

Procedure:

- While reviewing the Springboard, explain that *by doing this exercise, the student(s) were creating their ideas of a perfect place to live*. Go on to explain that *authors often create utopian societies such as these in literature.* (*Review terms.*) Tell the student(s) that *in this lesson they will read a story and determine whether the society created by the author is utopian or dystopian.*
- Distribute "Harrison Bergeron" and "R U 4 Real?" Have the student(s) work individually, in pairs, or small groups to read the story and complete the analysis form. (*Answers will vary, as the idea of utopia is very subjective. Some students may see the forced equality as a utopian idea, while others may see the handicapping in the story as a horrible procedure. Answers should be reasoned and spark discussion.)*
- Have the student(s) share and compare their ideas and discuss.

DIRECTIONS: Imagine the world as a perfect place and complete the graphic organizer telling how you envision each category in its perfection.

Society:

Environment:

In a Perfect World ...

Daily Life:

Government & Laws:

Harrison Bergeron

By Kurt Vonnegut Jr.

The year was 2081, and everybody was finally equal. They weren't only equal before God and the law. They were equal every which way. Nobody was smarter than anybody else. Nobody was better looking than anybody else. Nobody was stronger or quicker than anybody else. All this equality was due to the 211th, 212th, and 213th Amendments to the Constitution, and to the unceasing vigilance of agents of the United States Handicapper General.

Some things about living still weren't quite right, though. April, for instance, still drove people crazy by not being springtime. And it was in that clammy month that the H-G men took George and Hazel Bergeron's fourteen-year-old son, Harrison, away.

It was tragic, all right, but George and Hazel couldn't think about it very hard. Hazel had a perfectly average intelligence, which meant she couldn't think about anything except in short bursts. And George, while his intelligence was way above normal, had a little mental handicap radio in his ear. He was required by law to wear it at all times. It was tuned to a government transmitter. Every twenty seconds or so, the transmitter would send out some sharp noise to keep people like George from taking unfair advantage of their brains.

George and Hazel were watching television. There were tears on Hazel's cheeks, but she'd forgotten for the moment what they were about.

On the television screen were ballerinas.

A buzzer sounded in George's head. His thoughts fled in panic, like bandits from a burglar alarm.

"That was a real pretty dance, that dance they just did," said Hazel.

"Huh?" said George.

"That dance – it was nice," said Hazel.

"Yup," said George. He tried to think a little about the ballerinas. They weren't really very good – no better than anybody else would have been, anyway. They were burdened with sashweights and bags of birdshot, and their faces were masked, so that no one, seeing a free and graceful gesture or a pretty face, would feel like something the cat drug in. George was toying with the vague notion that maybe dancers shouldn't be handicapped. But he didn't get very far with it before another noise in his ear radio scattered his thoughts.

George winced. So did two out of the eight ballerinas.

Hazel saw him wince. Having no mental handicap herself she had to ask George what the latest sound had been.

"Sounded like somebody hitting a milk bottle with a ball peen hammer," said George.

"I'd think it would be real interesting, hearing all the different sounds," said Hazel, a little envious. "All the things they think up."

"Um," said George.

"Only, if I was Handicapper General, you know what I would do?" said Hazel. Hazel, as a matter of fact, bore a strong resemblance to the Handicapper General, a woman named Diana Moon Glampers. "If I was Diana Moon Glampers," said Hazel, "I'd have chimes on Sunday – just chimes. Kind of in honor of religion."

"I could think, if it was just chimes," said George.

"Well – maybe make 'em real loud," said Hazel. "I think I'd make a good Handicapper General."

"Good as anybody else," said George.

"Who knows better'n I do what normal is?" said Hazel.

"Right," said George. He began to think glimmeringly about his abnormal son who was now in jail, about Harrison, but a twenty-one-gun salute in his head stopped that.

"Boy!" said Hazel, "that was a doozy, wasn't it?"

It was such a doozy that George was white and trembling and tears stood on the rims of his red eyes. Two of the eight ballerinas had collapsed to the studio floor, were holding their temples.

"All of a sudden you look so tired," said Hazel. "Why don't you stretch out on the sofa, so's you can rest your handicap bag on the pillows, honeybunch." She was referring to the forty-seven pounds of birdshot in canvas bag, which was padlocked around George's neck. "Go on and rest the bag for a little while," she said. "I don't care if you're not equal to me for a while."

George weighed the bag with his hands. "I don't mind it," he said. "I don't notice it any more. It's just a part of me.

"You been so tired lately – kind of wore out," said Hazel. "If there was just some way we could make a little hole in the bottom of the bag, and just take out a few of them lead balls. Just a few."

"Two years in prison and two thousand dollars fine for every ball I took out," said George. "I don't call that a bargain."

"If you could just take a few out when you came home from work," said Hazel. "I mean – you don't compete with anybody around here. You just set around."

"If I tried to get away with it," said George, "then other people'd get away with it and pretty soon we'd be right back to the dark ages again, with everybody competing against everybody else. You wouldn't like that, would you?"

"I'd hate it," said Hazel.

"There you are," said George. "The minute people start cheating on laws, what do you think happens to society?"

If Hazel hadn't been able to come up with an answer to this question, George couldn't have supplied one. A siren was going off in his head.

"Reckon it'd fall all apart," said Hazel.

"What would?" said George blankly.

"Society," said Hazel uncertainly. "Wasn't that what you just said?"

"Who knows?" said George.

The television program was suddenly interrupted for a news bulletin. It wasn't clear at first as to what the bulletin was about, since the announcer, like all announcers, had a serious speech impediment. For about half a minute, and in a state of high excitement, the announcer tried to say, "Ladies and gentlemen – "

He finally gave up, handed the bulletin to a ballerina to read.

"That's all right –" Hazel said of the announcer, "he tried. That's the big thing. He tried to do the best he could with what God gave him. He should get a nice raise for trying so hard."

"Ladies and gentlemen" said the ballerina, reading the bulletin. She must have been extraordinarily beautiful, because the mask she wore was hideous. And it was easy to see that she was the strongest and most graceful of all the dancers, for her handicap bags were as big as those worn by two-hundred-pound men.

And she had to apologize at once for her voice, which was a very unfair voice for a woman to use. Her voice was a warm, luminous, timeless melody. "Excuse me – " she said, and she began again, making her voice absolutely uncompetitive.

"Harrison Bergeron, age fourteen," she said in a grackle squawk, "has just escaped from jail, where he was held on suspicion of plotting to overthrow the government. He is a genius and an athlete, is under–handicapped, and should be regarded as extremely dangerous."

A police photograph of Harrison Bergeron was flashed on the screen – upside down, then sideways, upside down again, then right side up. The picture showed the full length of Harrison against a background calibrated in feet and inches. He was exactly seven feet tall.

The rest of Harrison's appearance was Halloween and hardware. Nobody had ever worn heavier handicaps. He had outgrown hindrances faster than the H–G men could think them up. Instead of a little ear radio for a mental handicap, he wore a tremendous pair of earphones, and spectacles with thick wavy lenses. The spectacles were intended to make him not only half blind, but to give him whanging headaches besides.

Scrap metal was hung all over him. Ordinarily, there was a certain symmetry, a military neatness to the handicaps issued to strong people, but Harrison looked like a walking junkyard. In the race of life, Harrison carried three hundred pounds.

And to offset his good looks, the H–G men required that he wear at all times a red rubber ball for a nose, keep his eyebrows shaved off, and cover his even white teeth with black caps at snaggle–tooth random.

"If you see this boy," said the ballerina, "do not – I repeat, do not – try to reason with him."

There was the shriek of a door being torn from its hinges.

Screams and barking cries of consternation came from the television set. The photograph of Harrison Bergeron on the screen jumped again and again, as though dancing to the tune of an earthquake.

George Bergeron correctly identified the earthquake, and well he might have – for many was the time his own home had danced to the same crashing tune. "My God," said George, "that must be Harrison!"

The realization was blasted from his mind instantly by the sound of an automobile collision in his head.

When George could open his eyes again, the photograph of Harrison was gone. A living, breathing Harrison filled the screen.

Clanking, clownish, and huge, Harrison stood in the center of the studio. The knob of the uprooted studio door was still in his hand. Ballerinas, technicians, musicians, and announcers cowered on their knees before him, expecting to die.

"I am the Emperor!" cried Harrison. "Do you hear? I am the Emperor! Everybody must do what I say at once!" He stamped his foot and the studio shook.

"Even as I stand here –" he bellowed, "crippled, hobbled, sickened – I am a greater ruler than any man who ever lived! Now watch me become what I *can* become!"

Harrison tore the straps of his handicap harness like wet tissue paper, tore straps guaranteed to support five thousand pounds.

Harrison's scrap–iron handicaps crashed to the floor.

Harrison thrust his thumbs under the bar of the padlock that secured his head harness. The bar snapped like celery. Harrison smashed his headphones and spectacles against the wall.

He flung away his rubber–ball nose, revealed a man that would have awed Thor, the god of thunder.

"I shall now select my Empress!" he said, looking down on the cowering people. "Let the first woman who dares rise to her feet claim her mate and her throne!"

A moment passed, and then a ballerina arose, swaying like a willow.

Harrison plucked the mental handicap from her ear, snapped off her physical handicaps with marvelous delicacy. Last of all, he removed her mask.

She was blindingly beautiful.

"Now" said Harrison, taking her hand, "shall we show the people the meaning of the word dance? Music!" he commanded.

The musicians scrambled back into their chairs, and Harrison stripped them of their handicaps, too. "Play your best," he told them, "and I'll make you barons and dukes and earls."

The music began. It was normal at first – cheap, silly, false. But Harrison snatched two musicians from their chairs, waved them like batons as he sang the music as he wanted it played. He slammed them back into their chairs.

The music began again and was much improved.

Harrison and his Empress merely listened to the music for a while – listened gravely, as though synchronizing their heartbeats with it.

They shifted their weights to their toes.

Harrison placed his big hands on the girl's tiny waist, letting her sense the weightlessness that would soon be hers.

And then, in an explosion of joy and grace, into the air they sprang!

Not only were the laws of the land abandoned, but the law of gravity and the laws of motion as well.

They reeled, whirled, swiveled, flounced, capered, gamboled, and spun.

They leaped like deer on the moon.

The studio ceiling was thirty feet high, but each leap brought the dancers nearer to it. It became their obvious intention to kiss the ceiling.

They kissed it.

And then, neutralizing gravity with love and pure will, they remained suspended in air inches below the ceiling, and they kissed each other for a long, long time.

It was then that Diana Moon Glampers, the Handicapper General, came into the studio with a double-barreled ten-gauge shotgun. She fired twice, and the Emperor and the Empress were dead before they hit the floor.

Diana Moon Glampers loaded the gun again. She aimed it at the musicians and told them they had ten seconds to get their handicaps back on.

It was then that the Bergerons' television tube burned out.

Hazel turned to comment about the blackout to George.

But George had gone out into the kitchen for a can of beer.

George came back in with the beer, paused while a handicap signal shook him up. And then he sat down again. "You been crying?" he said to Hazel.

"Yup," she said,

"What about?" he said.

"I forget," she said. "Something real sad on television."

"What was it?" he said.

"It's all kind of mixed up in my mind," said Hazel.

"Forget sad things," said George.

"I always do," said Hazel.

"That's my girl," said George. He winced. There was the sound of a riveting gun in his head.

"Gee – I could tell that one was a doozy," said Hazel.

"You can say that again," said George.

"Gee –" said Hazel, "I could tell that one was a doozy."

R U 4 Real?

Utopian Ideas from the Story	Dystopian Ideas from the Story

Overall, do you think the society in the story was utopian or dystopian? Why?

Why do you think authors would seek to create utopian societies in their stories?

Do you think it's possible for an actual utopian society to exist? Why or why not?

I Have a Dream

Springboard:
Students should read "I Hear America Singing" and answer the questions.

Objective: The student will be able to describe the American dream theme in literature and other works.

Materials:
I Hear America Singing (Springboard handout)
I Have a Dream (3-page handout)
Dream Analysis (handout)

Terms to know:
American dream - the idea that anyone can become successful in America, regardless of who they are or where they come from
civil rights - fair and equal protection and treatment of all citizens

Procedure:
- While discussing the Springboard, have the student(s) generate definitions of the "American dream." *(Answers may vary, but it generally relates to the idea that anyone, regardless of his/her station in life, can become rich and/or successful.)* Go on to explain that *this lesson takes a closer look at the American Dream by examining a speech by a famous American, Dr. Martin Luther King, Jr.*
- Distribute "I Have a Dream" and have the student(s) read the speech, highlighting portions that they think are part of Dr. King's "dream." (*Answers will vary, but King dreamed of freedom, justice, brotherhood, a society where racial diversity did not mean inequality, etc.)*
- **EXTENSION**: Find an audio recording of Dr. King's speech and play it while the student(s) read along.
- Invite the student(s) to share what they highlighted and then distribute "Dream Analysis." Have the student(s) work independently, in pairs or small groups to complete the organizer.
- The student(s) should then share/compare their answers and discuss. *(Answers will vary, but they should be thoughtful and spark discussion.)*

I Hear America Singing

By Walt Whitman

I HEAR America singing, the varied carols I hear;
Those of mechanics – each one singing his, as it should be, blithe and strong;
The carpenter singing his, as he measures his plank or beam,
The mason singing his, as he makes ready for work, or leaves off work;
The boatman singing what belongs to him in his boat –
the deckhand singing on the steamboat deck;
The shoemaker singing as he sits on his bench – the hatter singing as he stands;
The wood-cutter's song – the ploughboy's, on his way in the morning,
or at the noon intermission, or at sundown;
The delicious singing of the mother – or of the young wife at work – or of the girl
sewing or washing – each singing what belongs to her, and to none else;
The day what belongs to the day –
At night, the party of young fellows, ***robust***, friendly,
Singing, with open mouths, their strong melodious songs.

The "songs" of Whitman's America are the
- A. ideas of educated professionals.
- B. thoughts of struggling workers.
- C. longings of the tradesmen.
- D. lives of ordinary people.

Which word is a synonym for "robust" in the poem?
- A. strong
- B. wealthy
- C. exhausted
- D. weary

Which word best describes Whitman's tone?
- A. melancholy
- B. angry
- C. proud
- D. bored

Choose one person mentioned in the poem and explain what you think his/her "dream" might be; what you think that person hopes and wishes for?

I Hear America Singing - Answers & Explanations

By Walt Whitman

I HEAR America singing, the varied carols I hear;
Those of mechanics – each one singing his, as it should be, blithe and strong;
The carpenter singing his, as he measures his plank or beam,
The mason singing his, as he makes ready for work, or leaves off work;
The boatman singing what belongs to him in his boat –
the deckhand singing on the steamboat deck;
The shoemaker singing as he sits on his bench – the hatter singing as he stands;
The wood-cutter's song – the ploughboy's, on his way in the morning,
or at the noon intermission, or at sundown;
The delicious singing of the mother – or of the young wife at work – or of the girl
sewing or washing – each singing what belongs to her, and to none else;
The day what belongs to the day –
At night, the party of young fellows, ***robust***, friendly,
Singing, with open mouths, their strong melodious songs.

The "songs" of Whitman's America are the

A. ideas of educated professionals.
B. thoughts of struggling workers.
C. longings of the tradesmen.
D. lives of ordinary people. *

(Choice A is false since no one mentioned is a "professional." C is false because not all people in the passage are tradesmen. D is the best answer, as the characters do not seem to be struggling; they're singing!)

Which word is a synonym for "robust" in the poem?

A. strong * C. exhausted
B. wealthy D. weary

(Choice B doesn't make sense; and C and D mean the same thing. By process of elimination and substituting the terms, students should be able to determine that Choice A is the best answer.)

Which word **BEST** describes Whitman's tone?

A. melancholy C. proud *
B. angry D. bored

(Whitman seems to be celebrating the people in the poem, which makes C the best choice.)

Choose one person mentioned in the poem and explain what you think his/her "dream" might be; what you think that person hopes and wishes for? ***Answers will vary, but should be well-reasoned.***

"I Have A DREAM"

BACKGROUND: The civil rights leader and minister, Dr. Martin Luther King Jr., gave a historic speech on August 28, 1963 on the steps of the Lincoln Memorial in Washington, D.C. The speech was the high point of a rally following the March on Washington by 300,000 or so people, mostly African American, demonstrating their support for civil rights legislation.

DIRECTIONS: Read Dr. King's famed speech, highlighting the parts describing his "dream."

"I am happy to join with you today in what will go down in history as the greatest demonstration for freedom in the history of our nation.

Five score years ago, a great American, in whose symbolic shadow we stand today, signed the Emancipation Proclamation. This momentous decree came as a great beacon light of hope to millions of Negro slaves who had been seared in the flames of withering injustice. It came as a joyous daybreak to end the long night of their captivity.

But one hundred years later, the Negro still is not free. One hundred years later, the life of the Negro is still sadly crippled by the manacles of segregation and the chains of discrimination. One hundred years later, the Negro lives on a lonely island of poverty in the midst of a vast ocean of material prosperity. One hundred years later, the Negro is still languishing in the corners of American society and finds himself an exile in his own land. So we have come here today to dramatize a shameful condition.

In a sense we have come to our nation's capital to cash a check. When the architects of our republic wrote the magnificent words of the Constitution and the Declaration of Independence, they were signing a promissory note to which every American was to fall heir. This note was a promise that all men, yes, black men as well as white men, would be guaranteed the unalienable rights of life, liberty, and the pursuit of happiness.

It is obvious today that America has defaulted on this promissory note insofar as her citizens of color are concerned. Instead of honoring this sacred obligation, America has given the Negro people a bad check, a check which has come back marked "insufficient funds." But we refuse to believe that the bank of justice is bankrupt. We refuse to believe that there are insufficient funds in the great vaults of opportunity of this nation. So we have come to cash this check — a check that will give us upon demand the riches of freedom and the security of justice. We have also come to this hallowed spot to remind America of the fierce urgency of now. This is no time to engage in the luxury of cooling off or to take the tranquilizing drug of gradualism. Now is the time to make real the promises of democracy. Now is the time to rise from the dark and desolate valley of segregation to the sunlit path of racial justice. Now is the time to lift our nation from the quick sands of racial injustice to the solid rock of brotherhood. Now is the time to make justice a reality for all of God's children.

It would be fatal for the nation to overlook the urgency of the moment. This sweltering summer of the Negro's legitimate discontent will not pass until there is an invigorating autumn of freedom and equality. Nineteen sixty-three is not an end, but a beginning. Those who hope that the Negro needed to blow off steam and will now be content will have a rude awakening if the nation returns to business as usual. There will be neither rest nor tranquility in America until the Negro is granted his citizenship rights. The whirlwinds of revolt will continue to shake the foundations of our nation until the bright day of justice emerges.

But there is something that I must say to my people who stand on the warm threshold which leads into the palace of justice. In the process of gaining our rightful place we must not be guilty of wrongful deeds. Let us not seek to satisfy our thirst for freedom by drinking from the cup of bitterness and hatred.

We must forever conduct our struggle on the high plane of dignity and discipline. We must not allow our creative protest to degenerate into physical violence. Again and again we must rise to the majestic heights of meeting physical force with soul force. The marvelous new militancy which has engulfed the Negro community must not lead us to a distrust of all white people, for many of our white brothers, as evidenced by their presence here today, have come to realize that their destiny is tied up with our destiny. They have come to realize that their freedom is inextricably bound to our freedom. We cannot walk alone.

As we walk, we must make the pledge that we shall always march ahead. We cannot turn back. There are those who are asking the devotees of civil rights, "When will you be satisfied?" We can never be satisfied as long as the Negro is the victim of the unspeakable horrors of police brutality. We can never be satisfied, as long as our bodies, heavy with the fatigue of travel, cannot gain lodging in the motels of the highways and the hotels of the cities. We cannot be satisfied as long as the Negro's basic mobility is from a smaller ghetto to a larger one. We can never be satisfied as long as our children are stripped of their selfhood and robbed of their dignity by signs stating "For Whites Only". We cannot be satisfied as long as a Negro in Mississippi cannot vote and a Negro in New York believes he has nothing for which to vote. No, no, we are not satisfied, and we will not be satisfied until justice rolls down like waters and righteousness like a mighty stream.

I am not unmindful that some of you have come here out of great trials and tribulations. Some of you have come fresh from narrow jail cells. Some of you have come from areas where your quest for freedom left you battered by the storms of persecution and staggered by the winds of police brutality. You have been the veterans of creative suffering. Continue to work with the faith that unearned suffering is redemptive.

Go back to Mississippi, go back to Alabama, go back to South Carolina, go back to Georgia, go back to Louisiana, go back to the slums and ghettos of our northern cities, knowing that somehow this situation can and will be changed. Let us not wallow in the valley of despair.

I say to you today, my friends, so even though we face the difficulties of today and tomorrow, I still have a dream. It is a dream deeply rooted in the American dream.

I have a dream that one day this nation will rise up and live out the true meaning of its creed: “We hold these truths to be self-evident; that all men are created equal.”

I have a dream that one day on the red hills of Georgia the sons of former slaves and the sons of former slave owners will be able to sit down together at the table of brotherhood.

I have a dream that one day even the state of Mississippi, a state sweltering with the heat of injustice, sweltering with the heat of oppression, will be transformed into an oasis of freedom and justice.

I have a dream that my four little children will one day live in a nation where they will not be judged by the color of their skin but by the content of their character.

I have a dream today.

I have a dream that one day every valley shall be exalted, every hill and mountain shall be made low, the rough places will be made plain, and the crooked places will be made straight, and the glory of the Lord shall be revealed, and all flesh shall see it together.

This is our hope. This is the faith that I go back to the South with. With this faith we will be able to hew out of the mountain of despair a stone of hope. With this faith we will be able to transform the jangling discords of our nation into a beautiful symphony of brotherhood. With this faith we will be able to work together, to pray together, to struggle together, to go to jail together, to stand up for freedom together, knowing that we will be free one day.

This will be the day when all of God's children will be able to sing with a new meaning, "My country, 'tis of thee, sweet land of liberty, of thee I sing. Land where my fathers died, land of the pilgrim's pride, from every mountainside, let freedom ring."

And if America is to be a great nation this must become true. So let freedom ring from the prodigious hilltops of New Hampshire. Let freedom ring from the mighty mountains of New York. Let freedom ring from the heightening Alleghenies of Pennsylvania!

Let freedom ring from the snowcapped Rockies of Colorado!

Let freedom ring from the curvaceous slopes of California!

But not only that; let freedom ring from Stone Mountain of Georgia!

Let freedom ring from Lookout Mountain of Tennessee!

Let freedom ring from every hill and molehill of Mississippi. From every mountainside, let freedom ring.

And when this happens, when we allow freedom to ring, when we let it ring from every village and every hamlet, from every state and every city, we will be able to speed up that day when all of God's children, black men and white men, Jews and Gentiles, Protestants and Catholics, will be able to join hands and sing in the words of the old Negro spiritual, "Free at last! free at last! thank God Almighty, we are free at last!"

Dream Analysis

Do you believe the American dream is attainable for all Americans? Why or why not?

How is your idea of the American dream similar to and different from Dr. King's?

SIMILAR:

DIFFERENT:

How do you think the American dream may have changed over time?

Why do you suppose this theme is common in American literature and other writings?

Finding Religion

Springboard:
Students should complete "What Is the Meaning of This?"
(Answers will vary but should be reasonable and spark discussion.)

Objective: The student will be able to describe some common Biblical allusions in western literature.

Materials:
What Is the Meaning of This? (Springboard handout)
In the Bible (handout)
The Grapes of Wrath (handout)

Terms to know:
allusion - reference to an event or piece of literature
meek - timid, shy, gentle

Procedure:

- During discussion of the Springboard, explain that *all of the statements are phrases or references from the Bible. Such Biblical allusions (review term) are very common in western literature, as non-western literature often contains allusions from the Qu'ran or other religious texts.* Go on to explain that *in this lesson the student(s) will conduct some research to learn more about Biblical allusions.*

- Distribute "In the Bible." The student(s) should work independently or in pairs to briefly research the underlined Bible story in each expression and generate any examples they can think of from books or movies using elements of that story in some way.
- Have the student(s) share and compare their ideas.
- Distribute "The Grapes of Wrath" and explain that *this work by John Steinbeck contains MANY biblical allusions*. To provide the background to the passage explain that *Tom Joad, one of the characters in the excerpt the student(s) will read, recently witnessed the killing of Jim Casy, an ex-preacher who was killed for trying to unite the poor workers in the story. Joad realizes he cannot stand idly by witnessing injustice and explains this to his worried mother Ma Joad*.
- Have the student(s) read the excerpt individually or in pairs and make notes in the margin about passages they think might be allusions to religious teachings in the Bible or elsewhere. *(Answers may vary and include the difference between right and wrong; 10 Commandments; Golden Rule, the idea that everyone is equal in God's eyes; belief in Heaven and the presence of God all around; etc.)*
- Have the student(s) share and compare their ideas and discuss. They should understand that *Biblical or other allusions are not always clear to the reader; they are the author's reference and may or may not be obvious*.

WHAT IS THE MEANING OF THIS?

DIRECTIONS: Read each statement and explain in your own words what you think it means.

"Am I my brother's keeper?"

____

____

____

"This is like the blind leading the blind."

____

____

____

"Blessed are the meek, for they shall inherit the Earth."

____

____

____

"Man does not live by bread alone."

____

____

____

"It is easier for a camel to pass through the eye of a needle than a rich man to enter the kingdom of God."

____

____

____

"An eye for an eye, a tooth for a tooth."

____

____

____

"A leopard cannot change its spots."

____

____

____

In the Bible

STORY	SUMMARY
Finding the Ark of the covenant	
Wine flowing like at the wedding at Cana	
He has the patience of Job	
In a den of lions (Daniel in the lion's den)	
Like manna from Heaven	
A good Samaritan	
Loaves and fishes	
A regular Noah's Ark	
My brother's keeper (Cain and Abel)	
Forbidden fruit (the Tree of Knowledge)	
He has the wisdom of Solomon	
The kiss of Judas	

List as many books, movies, plays, etc. that you think allude to any of these or other Bible stories:

In the Bible
Suggestions for Answers

Story:	Summary:
Finding the Ark of the covenant	***It was a sacred wooden crate that holds the 10 Commandments. The Israelites took it with them when they were exiled from the Holy Lands.***
Wine flowing like at the wedding at Cana	***Considered the first miracle of Jesus; he attended a wedding where the host ran out of wine for the guests. So Jesus turned water into wine.***
He has the patience of Job	***A pious man, Job was tempted by Satan to see if he would renounce his belief in God. Job lost his family and his property, and then battled a terrible disease. Yet despite all, he would not curse God.***
In a den of lions (Daniel in the lion's den)	***Jealous advisors of the king locked Daniel in a den of lions. When the den was unsealed, Daniel was found unharmed and said he was protected by God.***
Like manna from Heaven	***When Moses led the Israelites from slavery in Egypt, they wandered in the desert, lacking food and water. To feed them, God sent down manna (a food) from heaven.***
A good Samaritan	***A man was robbed, stripped, and left for dead. He was ignored by a priest and another leader, but helped by a Samaritan (hated by the audience of Jesus – the Jews). It shows that people should show kindness to all people.***
Loaves and fishes	***Another miracle of Jesus. He was preaching in the countryside to 5000 people, who needed to eat. A small boy had only 5 loaves of bread and 2 fishes which Jesus used to feed the huge crowd.***
A regular Noah's Ark	***God ordered Noah to load the animals 2 by 2 and build a huge ship to survive the rains and floods he was going to send to show his anger at man for their wickedness. After the flood God promised never to destroy the earth again.***
My brother's keeper (Cain and Abel)	***It's the story of two sons of Adam and Eve. Cain was very jealous and selfish and killed his brother Abel – the first murder in the Bible.***
Forbidden fruit (the Tree of Knowledge)	***Adam and Eve were told by God not to eat fruit from the tree, but Eve was tempted by a serpent to do so. Then she convinces Adam to eat it, also. The fruit made them aware of their nakedness (sin), and they were thrown out of the Garden of Eden by God.***
He has the wisdom of Solomon	***Two women went to King Solomon, both claiming to be the mother of a baby. Solomon tells them to cut the baby in half. One woman agreed while the other refused. Solomon granted the baby to the woman who was willing to give up her baby to save its life.***
The kiss of Judas	***When the Roman soldiers came to arrest Jesus, Judas kissed him to identify him and was paid 30 silver pieces to betray him.***

List as many books, movies, plays, etc. that you think allude to any of these or other Bible stories: ***Possibilities include: Raiders of the Lost Ark, Evan Almighty, Harry Potter, The Day After Tomorrow, Armageddon, The Ten Commandments, etc.***

THE GRAPES OF WRATH

(an excerpt from the John Steinbeck novel)

Tom Joad: I been thinking about us too, about our people living like pigs and good rich land layin' fallow. Or maybe one guy with a million acres and a hundred thousand farmers starvin'. And I been wonderin' if all our folks got together and yelled –

Ma Joad: Tommy, they'd drag you out and cut you down just like they done to Casy.

Tom: They'd drag me anyways. Sooner or later they'll get me one way or another. Till then –

Ma: Tommy, you're not aimin' to kill anybody.

Tom: No, Ma, not that. That ain't it. Just, as long as I'm an outlaw anyways, maybe I can do something, just find out somethin', just scrounge around and maybe find out what it is that's wrong and see if they ain't somethin' that can be done about it. I ain't thought it out that clear, Ma. I can't. I don't know enough.

Ma: How am I gonna know about ya, Tommy? They could kill ya and I'd never know. They could hurt ya. How am I gonna know?

Tom: Maybe it's like Casy says. A fellow ain't got a soul of his own, just a little piece of a big soul, the one big soul that belongs to everybody, then –

Ma: Then what, Tom?

Tom: Then it don't matter. I'll be all around in the dark. I'll be everywhere, wherever you can look. Wherever there's a fight so hungry people can eat, I'll be there. Wherever there's a cop beatin' up a guy, I'll be there. I'll be in the way guys yell when they're mad. I'll be in the way kids laugh when they're hungry and they know supper's ready and where people are eatin' the stuff they raise and livin' in the houses they build. I'll be there too...

Ma: I don't understand it, Tom.

Tom: Me, neither Ma, but – just somethin' I been thinkin' about.

Coloring Books

Springboard:

Students should complete "My Favorite Colors."
(Answers will vary but should spark discussion.)

Objective: The student will be able to explain the meanings and symbolism associated with color.

Materials: My Favorite Colors (Springboard handout)
Color My World (handout)
True Colors (handout)

Terms to know: **associate** - connect things in the mind

Procedure:

- After reviewing the Springboard, explain that *in this lesson the student(s) will consider the various meanings of colors in literature and create a short story using colors to enhance it*.
- Distribute "Color My World" and have the student(s) work independently, in pairs, or small groups to read the information and apply what they learn to the questions. (*Answers will vary but should be reasonable based on handout information.)*
- Distribute "True Colors" and have the student(s) complete the analysis form using lesson information.
- Then have them share their answers and discuss how color can enhance a story or character. (*Answers will vary, but among other things, it can provide clues to a character or setting and make stories and characters more interesting.)*

My Favorite Colors

DIRECTIONS: Brainstorm lists of things, places, ideas, human characteristics, etc. that each of the following colors bring to mind? Then, answer the questions below.

YELLOW:

RED:

BLUE:

WHITE:

Why do you think we associate certain things with certain colors? How do you think our associations contribute to which colors are our "favorites?"

Color My World

DIRECTIONS: Study the list of colors and the meanings generally associated with each. Then, use the descriptions to answer the questions.

White: Positively associated with light, innocence, purity, and timelessness. Negatively associated with death, terror, the supernatural, and cosmic mystery.

Black: Positively associated with knowledge and intelligence or the ancient. Negatively associated with evil, sadness, chaos, mystery, the unknown, and death.

Yellow: Usually associated with sun, hope, and happiness.

Red: Depicts great passion in both love and violence. Red can also denote blood, sacrifice, or disorder.

Blue: Often associated with compromise, peace, calm, truth, security, and spiritual purity.

Green: Positively associated with life, rebirth, growth, hope, and fertility. Negatively associated with death and decay.

Purple: Often associated with power and loyalty.

Gold/Silver: Associated with wealth, status, and power.

---

1. Why do brides wear white? ______________________________

2. What color(s) do kings and queens usually wear? Why? ______________________________

3. What kind of women would wear red in a story? Why? ______________________________

4. In westerns, why do some guys wear white hats and others wear black ones? ______________________________

TRUE COLORS

DIRECTIONS: Using your knowledge of color meaning and symbolism, write a paragraph to explain the symbolic meaning of each of the following. Then on the back, draw one example of your own and explain its "colorful" symbolism.

A Red, White, and Blue Flag

Witch with a Green Face Dressed in Black

Easter Eggs in Assorted Pastel Colors

Bouquet of Red Roses with White Accents

Wrapping Up

Springboard:

Students should follow the directions to complete (individually or in groups) as much of the "Literary Links" as possible.

(Answer will vary.)

Objective: The student will identify and explain the themes of some of their favorite literary (or cinematic) works.

Materials: Literary Links (handout)
Read & Write (handout)

Procedure:

- During discussion of the Springboard, explain that *in this lesson the student will see how theme plays out in stories*.
- Distribute "Read & Write" and review the directions. The student(s) should then work individually, in pairs, or small groups to find and read at least one short story, or you can assign specific readings. They should read and complete the analysis form as instructed.
- Have the student(s) share / compare their analyses and discuss.

LITERARY LINKS

DIRECTIONS: Try to think of a book, short story, poem, movie, TV show, character in any of these, etc. that provides an example of each of the themes listed. Fill in the chart with as many as you can, and then try to think of ONE MORE theme that isn't listed to fill in the last line.

THEME	EXAMPLE
Acceptance	
Alienation	
Ambition	
American Dream	
Anger	
Betrayal	
Bravery	
Coming of Age	
Community	
Conformity	
Courage	
Cowardice	
Cycle of Life	
Determination	
Duty	
Faith	
Fate	
Freedom	
Friendship	
Grief	
Guilt	
Honor	
Individuality	
Inequality	
Isolation	
Jealousy	
Journeys	
Loneliness	
Loss of Innocence	
Love	
Loyalty	
Power of One	
Prejudice	
Personal Sacrifice	
Self-development	
Truth	

Read & Write

DIRECTIONS: Find a short story to read on the Internet or from another source. Read the story and complete the analysis below.

Title: ______________________________

Author: ______________ Source: ______________

What would you say are the theme(s) in the story? ______________

Explain your ideas and how the theme(s) play out. ______________

Do you think the author was able to address one or more themes clearly? Explain.

REVIEWING TERMS

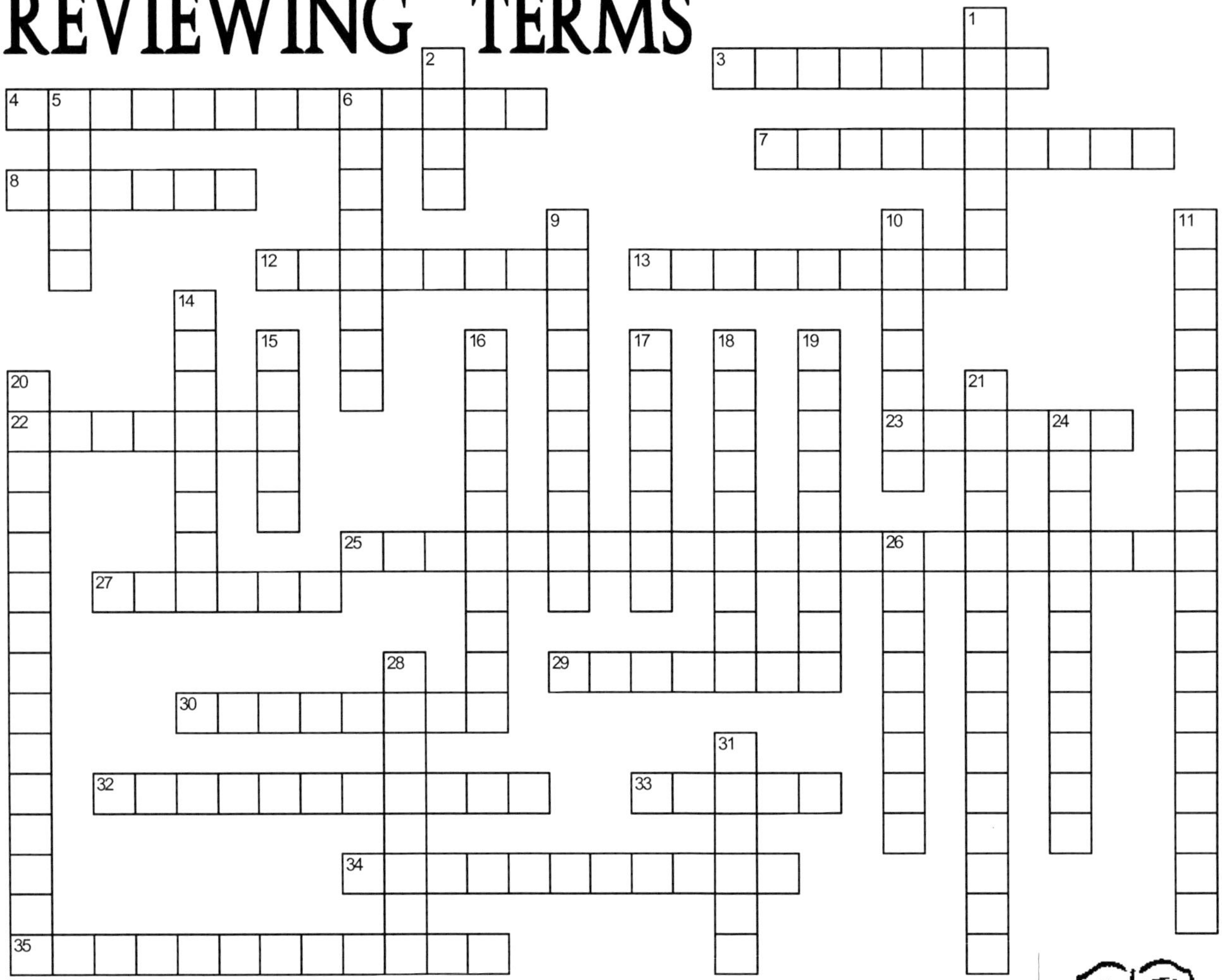

ACROSS

3 fighting among people of one nation
4 idea that anyone can succeed with hard work
7 moving from one life stage to another
8 perfect society
12 an introduction to a literary work
13 one who takes the blame for others
22 take care of
23 principles of right and wrong
25 hardships or painful experiences that test one's ability to carry on
27 teacher or guide to a younger or less experienced person
29 one who is guided by a mentor
30 prediction for the future
32 family members of a later time
33 unifying idea or subject of a story
34 thinker
35 that which cannot be explained

DOWN

1 low, protective wall
2 shy and gentle
5 a recurring pattern through time and place
6 horrible society of people living wretched lives
9 woman who tempts others
10 trip taken by a character to learn about himself/herself
11 forbidden romance theme in literature
14 reference to an event or piece of literature
15 search for something important
16 terrible treatment of others
17 a basic part of something
18 typical example or model
19 connect things in the mind
20 state of being unaware
21 defining qualities
24 protections and equal treatment of citizens
26 expected loser
28 describing something as something else
31 exaggerated story based loosely on historical facts

REVIEWING TERMS PUZZLE ANSWERS

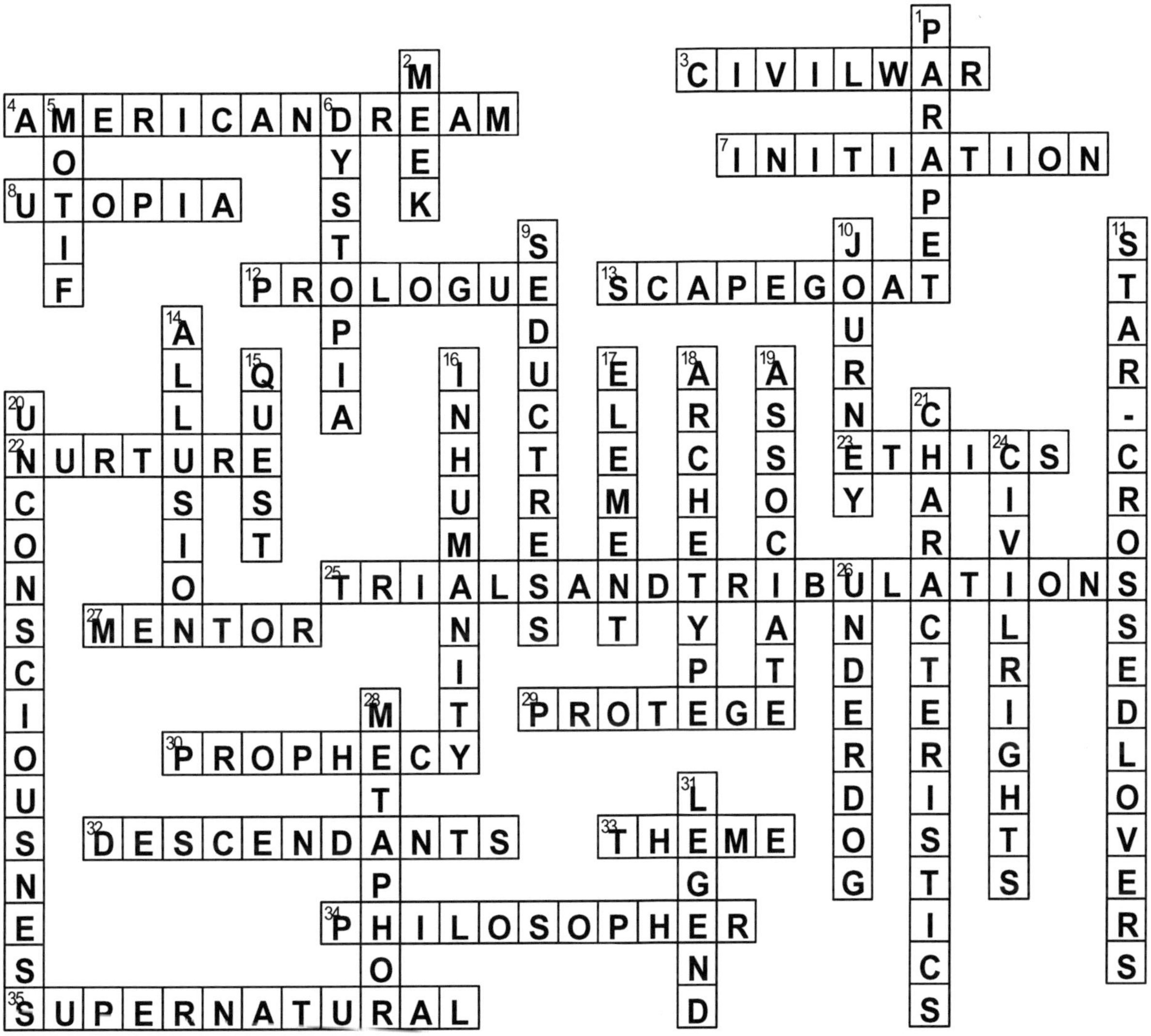

Literary Themes (A)

Matching - Write the letter of the correct definition in the blank:

1. ____ motif	A. exaggerated story based on fact
2. ____ underdog	B. introduction to a literary work
3. ____ descendant	C. expected loser of a fight
4. ____ supernatural	D. timid, weak
5. ____ legend	E. recurring pattern through time and place
6. ____ philosopher	F. horrible society where people live wretched lives
7. ____ nurture	G. thinker
8. ____ prologue	H. family member of a later time
9. ____ dystopia	I. to take care of and encourage
10. ____ meek	J. magical; something that cannot be explained

Give an example of each:

11. theme - ____________________

12. characteristic - ____________________

13. mentor - ____________________

14. inhumanity - ____________________

15. trials and tribulations - ____________________

Multiple Choice - Write the letter of the correct answer in the blank:

16. ____ Stories in which a character transitions from youth to adulthood are called
    A. underdog stories. C. coming of age stories.
    B. hero stories. D. adolescent stories.

17. ____ In journey stories characters would be <u>LEAST</u> likely to
    A. have a forbidden romance which would end in death.
    B. travel to places with enchanted and magical landscapes
    C. meet and possibly battle against dangerous creatures.
    D. go on a quest and have to face many trials and tribulations.

18. ____ Which Bible story is an example of the underdog theme?
    A. Daniel and the Lion's Den C. Adam and Eve
    B. David and Goliath D. Noah's Ark

19. ____ The nurturer, waif, temptress, and librarian are all examples of
    A. star-crossed lovers. C. supernatural legends.
    B. female archetypes. D. mentors to heroes.

Fully answer the following question:

20. Explain how color could be used as a symbol in a story.

Skills for Forms A-C:

The first thing you notice about Cruella DeVil is her spiky brittle hair split down the middle; white on one side, black on the other. Her sneering lips and icy stare makes your blood run cold. Her eyes bulge out of her head like she is ready to explode in anger at any moment, which she often does with her sidekicks, Horace and Jasper. Her body is rail-thin, each limb like a toothpick, yet she always dresses in skin tight satin gowns. What she most wants you to notice, though, is not her strange appearance, but her full length fur coat that covers her from her skinny neck to her pointy feet. She adores fur and cannot live without it. In fact the only thing she truly loves is fur, and she doesn't care what she has to do to get it. She's even willing to skin adorable Dalmatian puppies! Cruella DeVil lives a ***wretched*** *life, hating everyone and everything except fur coats.*

21. ____ Which literary them **BEST** describes this passage?
    A. the hero
    B. the underdog
    C. utopia
    D. inhumanity
22. ____ Which of these archetypes describes Cruella DeVil?
    A. the seductress
    B. the boss
    C. the waif
    D. the nurturer
23. ____ Which word is a synonym for "wretched"?
    A. miserable
    B. proud
    C. violent
    D. happy

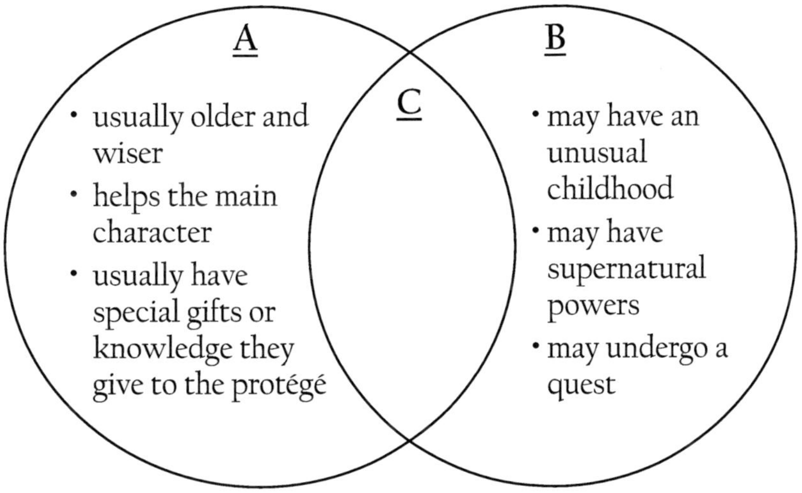

24. ____ In the graphic, "A" describes ____ and "B" describes ____.
    A. heroes ... mentors
    B. journeys ... heroes
    C. mentors ... journeys
    D. mentors ... heroes
25. ____ Which statement would **BEST FIT** in the part of the diagram labeled "C"?
    A. One describes men and the other women.
    B. Journeys are always to mysterious places.
    C. Neither makes a story more interesting.
    D. Both represent archetypes in literature.

Literary Themes (B)

Fill in the blanks with unit terms:

1. The most exciting ____________________ of the story was the surprise ending.
2. The Superbowl was an upset since the __________________________ team won.
3. Many African Americans are ____________________________________ of slaves.
4. The character had a ________________________ power to see through anything.
5. The ________________ of El Dorado tells of a South American tribal chief who covered himself in gold dust and dove into a river.
6. The ___________________ spent a lot of time thinking about the meaning of life.
7. The mother ______________________________ her children with love and care.
8. The _________________ at the beginning explained the background of the story.
9. In the book's ______________________ society, everyone was kind and well-fed.
10. The ________________ young boy was very timid and shy around other children.

Give an example of each:

11. protégé - ____
12. inhumanity -____
13. theme - ____
14. American Dream - ____
15. allusion - ____

Multiple Choice - Write the letter of the correct answer in the blank:

16. ____ Which statement would NOT be true of literary journeys?
    A. A main character visits fantastic places with enchanted landscapes.
    B. The story usually ends with the tragic death of the main character.
    C. Someone on a quest faces many trials and tribulations along the way.
    D. The main character may encounter dangerous or magical creatures.
17. ____ Coming of age stories MOST OFTEN involve
    A. the transition of an innocent child to adulthood.
    B. an innocent female character who is orphaned.
    C. star – crossed lovers who can never be together.
    D. an older and wiser mentor who helps the hero.
18. ____ The color that a character wears may be used to
    A. tell the story in a new and more exciting way.
    B. determine which person is the main character.
    C. give information about the character's personality.
    D. make an otherwise boring story more interesting.
19. ____ The waif, librarian and spunky kid are all examples of
    A. themes. B. archetypes. C. patterns. D. allusions.

Fully answer the following question on your own paper and attach:

20. Explain and give an example of an archetype in a story.

Literary Themes (C)

Complete the analogies with unit terms:

1. Buyer is to shopper, as student is to ______________________________.
2. Part is to a machine, as ______________________________ is to a story.
3. A moat is to a castle, as a/an ______________________________ is to a roof.
4. Perfection is to a building design, as ________________________ is to a society.
5. House is to home, as trait is to ______________________________.
6. Friend is to buddy, as co-worker is to ______________________________.
7. Teacher is to instruction, as ____________________________ is to thinking.
8. Forbearers are to earlier, as __________________________ are to later in time.
9. A simile uses "as" or "like," as a/an _______________________ uses "is" or "are."
10. Outgoing is to withdrawn, as assertive is to ___________________________.

Name each category:

11. freedom of speech, voting, equal treatment - ___________________________
12. nice home, successful career, happy family life - _________________________
13. torture, unfair imprisonment, murder - ________________________________
14. hunger, fighting enemies, exhaustion - ________________________________
15. coming of age, overcoming adversity, individuality - ____________________

Multiple Choice - Write the letter of the correct answer in the blank:

16. ____ All of these are examples of "initiations" EXCEPT
   A. a Jewish bar mitzvah.
   B. Saturday night out.
   C. high school graduation.
   D. a wedding ceremony.
17. ____ Which of these descriptions provides the BEST example of a seductress?
   A. She was tall and lean and her hips swayed side-to-side as she walked.
   B. The teenage girl leaned awoke and understood the horror of the crash.
   C. She was fierce, willing to do almost anything to get what she wanted.
   D. The old woman was weary from long years of suffering and loneliness.
18. ____ "He was dressed all in black from head to toe" MOST LIKELY
   A. is an allusion to a cowboy.
   B. suggests the supernatural.
   C. implies mystery or evil.
   D. is a metaphor for fear.
19. ____ Which of these characters is **the WORST example** of an archetype?
   A. an evil sorcerer
   B. a happy child
   C. an adoring grandmother
   D. a high-powered executive

Fully answer the following question on your own paper and attach:

20. Explain and give an example of the use of allusion in literature.

Literary Themes
Suggestions for Answers

Form A:

1. E
2. C
3. H
4. J
5. A
6. G
7. I
8. B
9. F
10. D
11. journey, greed, star-crossed lovers, inequality, etc.
12. eye color, height, personality, education, etc.
13. Obi-Wan Kenobi, Dumbledore, Charlotte, etc.
14. the Holocaust, Indian Removal, 9-11-01, murder, etc.
15. man-eating dragons, Cyclops, hunger, exhaustion, etc.
16. C
17. A
18. B
19. B
20. Answers will vary: the white gown for a wedding, black hat for a cowboy, grey day at a funeral, (with explanations) etc.

Form B:

1. element
2. underdog
3. descendants
4. supernatural
5. legend
6. philosopher
7. nurtured
8. prologue
9. utopian
10. meek
11. student, Wilbur, Grasshopper, Harry Potter, etc.
12. murder, genocide, Indian Removal, torture, etc.
13. journey, star-crossed lovers, redemption, coming of age, etc.
14. big house, nice cars, great job, happy family, etc.
15. Manna from Heaven, Fishes and Loaves, Noah's Ark, etc.
16. B
17. A
18. C
19. B
20. Answers may vary: evil sorceress, seductress, mad scientist, the boss, the waif, the nurturer, etc. (with descriptions).

Form C:

1. protégé
2. element
3. parapet
4. utopia
5. characteristic
6. associate
7. philosopher
8. descendants
9. metaphor
10. meek
21. civil rights
22. American Dream
23. inhumanity
24. trials and tribulations
25. themes
26. B
27. A
28. C
29. B
30. Answers may vary and include any reference to the Bible (such as loaves and fishes, manna from heaven, etc.) or other works of literature, movies, etc.

Skills for Forms A-C:

21. D
22. B
23. A
24. D
25. D

RESOURCES

www.orangeusd.k12.ca.us/yorba/literary elements.htm - Literary Elements. Yorba Middle School, Orange Unified School District, 2009.

www.howtodothings.com/hobbies/a4231-how-to-identify-literary-themes.html - "How to Identify Literary Themes." How To Do Things.com, 2009.

www3.delta.edu/drsnyder/CommonThemesInLiterature.html - "Common Themes in Literature." Daniel R. Snyder, editor, Delta College, 2006.

www.buzzle.com/articles/enduring-value-of-the-underdog-story.html - "The Enduring Value of an Underdog Story," buzzle.com, 2009.

classiclit.about.com/od/heroinliterature/Hero.htm - "Hero." About.com, 2009.

www.educationoasis.com/bc/articles/exploringheroes.htm - Heroes and Heroines in Children's Literature. The Education Oasis, 2009.

www.essortment.com/all/archetypesinli rfnd.htm - Archetypes in Literature, Film and Life. pagewise.com, 2009.

www.readprint.com/work-6619/Understanding-Literary-Archetypes-Nishank-Khanna - Khanna, Nishank. "Understanding Literary Archetypes." readprint.com, 2009.

www.uncp.edu/home/canada/work/allam/general/glossary.htm - Glossary of Literary Terms. University of North Carolina at Pembroke, 2009.

en.wikipedia.org/wiki/Star-crossed - "Star Crossed Lovers" Wikipedia, the free encyclopedia, Wikipedia.com, 2009.

www.greece.k12.ny.us/instruction/ela/6-12/reading/annotatedbib.htm - Multi-genre Thematic Literature Lists. Greece Central School District, 2009.

www.cloudnet.com/~edrbsass/edadolescentlit.htm - Lesson Plans and Resources for Young and Adolescent Literature, 2009.

nancykeane.com/rl/#Themes - ATN Book Lists by Theme. Nancy J. Keane, 2006.

classiclit.about.com/od/genresthemesinbooks/Genres Themes in Books.htm - Genres, Themes and Topics in Books. about.com, 2009.

I Think: Thematic Units

Some of our other **I Think** offerings include:

Series	Titles
I Think: Connections	Civilization, Democracy, Dictators, Ethnic Conflict, Indigenous People, Imperialism
I Think: U.S. History	Colonial America, American Revolution, Westward Expansion, The Civil War, Reconstruction Era, Problems & Progressives, The Modern Era, The African American Experience
I Think: Government	Electing the President, Civic Participation. The Constitution, The Executive, Legislative, and Judicial Branches
I Think: Geography	What Is Geography?, U.S. Regions, World Geography by Region
I Think: World History	A wide variety of Ancient Civilizations units, Middle Ages, Renaissance, the World Wars, The Holocaust, etc.
I Think: Economics	What Is Economics? Personal Finance
I Think: Reading & Writing	Poetry, Short Stories, Literary Themes, Novels, Biographies, etc.
I Think: I Can!	Early Learning Thematics
I Think: It's Elementary!	America's Colonies, Revolution, Economics, etc.

We're adding more titles all the time.
Check our websites for current listings!

www.inspirededucators.com